MEG SWANSEN'S

KNITTING

INTERWEAVE PRESS

Acknowledgements

Thank you to the following accomplished and patient people:

Editors Judith Durant, Dorothy Ratigan, and Ann Budd.

Photographer Joe Coca and his assistant, Lisa Rabold.

Book Designer Dean Howes and illustrator Gayle Ford.

Copy Editor Stephen Beal.

Models Cully Swansen and Lloie Schwartz, in addition to the pros—Frank, Amy, Geraldine, and Nikki.

And for the initial concept of doing a book at all: Linda Ligon and Jillian Moreno.

Cover design, Bren Frisch
Photography, Joe Coca
Technical editing, Dorothy T. Ratigan

Interweave Press
201 East Fourth Street
Loveland, Colorado 80537
USA

Library of Congress Cataloging-in-Publication Data:

Swanson, Meg. 1942–
    Meg Swansen's Knitting
        p.   cm.
    Includes index.
    ISBN 1-883010-58-6 (hardbound)
    1. Knitting patterns. 2. Sweaters. I. Title
TT825.S88 1999
746.43'20432—dc21   99-29404
                                    CIP

Printed in the United States of America
First printing: 7.5M:999:RRD

Contents

Introduction

WE LIVED IN A LOVELY OLD FOUR-STORY HOUSE in New Hope, Pennsylvania, on the banks of the Delaware River, having moved there from New York City where I was born. I was four or five when my mother Elizabeth Zimmermann taught me to knit . . . we were on the windowed porch overlooking the river and I stood next to her as she sat with her arms around me, guiding my hands through the natural awkwardness of learning a new skill. The first actual project I can remember was about four years later. We had moved from New Hope to Shorewood, Wisconsin, and I knitted a Christmas scarf for my Auntie Pete in England (she used to make us [my sister Lloie and me] beautiful smocks, soft beige or gray wool challis with white smocking. I never met her. As a first-generation American I have met very few of my relatives). My scarf for Auntie Pete was a typical, narrow garter-stitch strip with stripes of color and after about eight inches my mother suggested that I might like to curve the back of the neck to make a more anatomical horseshoe shape and she showed me how to work short rows. This was long before the advent of "wrapping" and I'm sure we used Mary Thomas's recommendation to slip the first stitch after turning. I was quite pleased with myself.

Sometime during third grade, I was kicked out of Brownies for general rowdiness. And it was the very day that my mother was to be a surprise guest and talk to us little girls about knitting. I dawdled the long way home as I attempted to make my arrival coincide with the usual after-Brownie-meeting time. As I came in the door and began to prevaricate, I noticed that Ma was unsuccessfully hiding a smile; she knew I had been booted out of Brownies and, as I recall, she didn't mind much. We were never great joiners. I think it had to do with being new Americans; with no relatives in the United States, our family of five drew the wagons into a circle.

My knitting life was very sporadic for the next

Zimmermann home in New Hope, Pennsylvania, 1945.

decade or so until near the end of high school when I knitted a sweater for a boyfriend: It was loden green with a plain, hemmed body and cabled cuff-to-cuff sleeves/yoke.

Facilitated by my high school art teacher and friend Harold Huber, I arranged barters with several other artists, swapping sweaters for paintings. Barter is a wonderful method of exchange; each craftsperson admires the work of the other and, usually, keeping money out of the transaction seems to elevate it to another level and help each participant feel they have gotten the best of the bargain.

While I was in high school, my mother started the mail-order knitting-supply business that is now called Schoolhouse Press. She was tired of having her circular designs "edited" into flat pieces by magazines and she was flush with the success of having knitted, on commission for *Vogue*, the very first set of Aran instructions available in the United States. (They appeared in the Feb/Mar 1957 *Vogue*

Pattern Book.) In lieu of payment, *Vogue* listed Elizabeth as the source for the natural, unbleached wool with which to knit the beautiful sweater. This combination of events led her to publish Newsletter #1, which was mailed in September 1958. It contained her design for a Fair Isle patterned yoke sweater, knitted in Shetland wool, which she began, gingerly, to import from the Shetland Isles.

Elizabeth had also taped "The Busy Knitter," an instructional series for public television (taking the cat, Kline, to the studio with her), which was being aired around the country, and her mail-order business was under way. My friend Ninka Hainer and I would sit at the dining-room table and peel quarters off tottering stacks of letters requesting the study guides that backed up the TV series. Elizabeth was never enamored of the name given to her program, so when she made the second series a few years later, she saw an opportunity to brighten it up by calling it "The Busy Knitter Rides Again." PBS wouldn't let her and the title became "The Busy Knitter II." (Both series have been lost forever. Even though they were kept in the PBS vaults in Washington, D.C., over the decades the tapes suffered from dropout and were destroyed.)

It was through a knitting customer of Elizabeth's that my sister Lloie and I got our first ski-resort jobs. Maryanne and Don Pfeiffle were building the very first inn at the newly developed Sugarloaf Mountain ski area in northern Maine, and in casual correspondence with my mother mentioned that they were looking for employees. Lloie and I flew out to become ski bums for

> **MY PARENTS WERE** philosophically opposed to television and we had never owned one. When my mother's TV shows were being aired, she *rented* a set for thirteen weeks.

> **MY THIRD-GRADE TEACHER,** Miss Weeks, was one of my two all-time favorites. I tried to contact her after high school, but to no avail. Recently, after forty-six years, I received a note from her and we met again. She (now Mrs. Brown) remembered me as more "spirited" than "trouble-maker".
>
> Nearly all of my report cards, grades three through six, had a variation of the same remark: "Meggie sacrifices accuracy for speed." My knitting often suffers from the same character flaw.

the season. In those days the airlines levied a penalty for checking luggage that weighed more than forty pounds. Our ski boots weighed nearly that all by themselves, so we brilliantly decided to wear them for the trip. I well remember the five-hour delay at Logan airport in Boston, and the pain. We finally boarded a tiny plane to I-can't-remember-where. We were met at the airport—which turned out all its lights as we drove away—and taken to the Sugarloaf Inn, the front entrance of which was still under construction. In the pitch dark, in our ski boots, in a snowstorm, we climbed a steep and slippery ladder up to the dining room on the second floor and met Maryanne and Don.

Elizabeth with Thomas, Meg, and Lloie. Lloie and I are wearing garter-stitch jackets; we all have on knitted stockings.

We spent an ideal winter working as waitresses in exchange for our room, board, and season lift tickets. We had to serve only breakfast and dinner and we skied every day, all day. The guests called us Neenah and Menasha because we were sisters from Wisconsin (those are sister cities near Green Bay, Wisconsin.) We had a panoply of magnificent sweaters from our Ma, which gave us great dash on the mountain and aprés-ski, but little incentive to do any knitting of our own.

"Ski Bums" of Sugarloaf Mountain. That's me on the left with Pam Gary and Lloie.

My FIRST TRANS-atlantic trip was by ship when I was fifteen and Lloie and I sailed from New York City to Southampton. Lloie continued on to visit a friend in Germany and I spent the summer in England meeting my maternal relatives for the first time. I sailed home alone in time for school.

During that winter the U.S. ski team came to Sugarloaf and we met Dave McCoy, coach of the team and owner of Mammoth Mountain ski resort in the Sierra Nevadas of California. He invited us to come west next winter and that is just what we did, getting a Drive-Away Car from Chicago. I remember a pink Thunderbird sports car; Lloie says it was gray. This time we were lift-ticket sellers, working alternate mornings and weekends in exchange for room, board, and season lift tickets. It was during that second winter of ski-bumming that I was hit with a strong urge to knit and made several sweaters, including one of Elizabeth's classics: a Three and One Sweater. The Three and One is a beautiful allover color pattern comprised of three stitches of one color and one stitch of the other. It is a lovely and soothing—almost hypnotic—rhythm to knit. That was in 1962 and the impulse to knit has not abandoned me since.

When the ski season ended, Lloie stayed in the mountains, got married, and she and Stoo became certified ski instructors at Mammoth. I set off to attend an art school in Germany, the *Blocherer Schule*, living in Pasing with my Aunt Traudl and her three sons and taking the train into Munich

THE DAY AFTER GRADUATING FROM Milwaukee University School, I flew to Los Angeles and spent the next four years traveling and working. One gig was as an information operator for General Telephone in Santa Monica. It became boring fairly quickly (except when people called for information like "Do you bake the pie *before* adding the meringue?" and "How do you spell 'awkward'?"), but things looked up when another operator and I were chosen to run the phones set up in the lobby of the Civic Center during the week of rehearsal that preceded the televised Academy Awards. Frank Sinatra was the master of ceremonies that year and I had to deliver messages to him and to Sophia Loren. Ethel Merman came sweeping into the lobby one day, handed me a piece of paper with a phone number on it, and commanded, "Get me Irving Berlin in Palm Springs!" She stood behind me, and when the connection was made, grabbed my headset and bellowed into it, "HALLO, IRVING?"

My sweaters were featured in the October 1970 issue of Woman's Day.

many, many years until Reynolds picked up this splendid exotic fiber for the mass U.S. market and called it Lopi. But they didn't trust U.S. knitters not to panic at the fact that the wool was a roving and could be pulled apart easily, so they spun it gently.

The "discovery" of Icelandic wool was a kind of turning point that charged and strengthened my love of knitting. I had met my future husband Chris the summer before Lloie and I went to Mammoth, and as he and I zigged and zagged around the world on different paths, meeting occasionally and writing to each other continuously, I knitted him a number of sweaters. We were married in 1964 and moved to West 73rd Street in New York City (between Amsterdam and Central Park West) where I began to knit sweaters on commission for some of the musicians Chris worked with. I remember a honey-colored, V-Neck Aran cardigan for Stan Getz, an Icelandic pullover for Gary Burton, and a Shetland Wool tie for Gene Cherico.

When we moved out of the city a few years later, I opened a small wool shop in the living room of our house in New Hope, Pennsylvania—yes, the same house on the Delaware River where I first learned to knit. My parents had perspicaciously held onto it. Chris was working with Phil Woods, who also lived in New Hope, and it was our mutual love of knitting as well as of music that caused Phil's wife, Chan Parker, and me to become great friends. (Chan is the widow of Charlie

each morning. I became friends with two other students, Hanna Gunnarsdottir from Iceland and Maya Oesch from Switzerland. During school holidays I spent a week in Lausanne with Maya, and later visited Hanna's family in Reykjavik for three weeks. Iceland is amazingly beautiful, Icelanders are splendid, and I had a wonderful time but, uff! The *Icelandic wool*: unspun, undyed and put up in great twelve-ounce wheels (or "cheeses" as some Icelanders called them). This beautiful and unique fiber was totally unknown in the United States at the time and I became captivated by it (still am). I knitted a sweater in Iceland (a dark brown pullover in mistake-stitch rib) and shipped a great bundle of wool back to Elizabeth who began to import it in 1962 or '63. We were voices in the wilderness for

> **THE DRIVE TO** California with Lloie was my first of three crossings on Route 66. The second time was with Chris, from LA to Chicago, during a two-week break he had from the Stan Kenton band. The third trip was with Diane Peterson. In 1960 she and I had both been sales "girls" in LA at a Lanz of California shop on the corner of Wilshire and Fairfax. Then in 1963, we were information operators at the phone company in Santa Monica. She was also a good knitting buddy and we drove, eventually, to New York City in my very first car, Flash.

Cully and Liesl, 1974. Cully is going on his first camping trip.

Parker and their life together was the subject of Clint Eastwood's 1989 movie *Bird*.) She knitted a slew of beautiful sweaters for Phil and their children and we hung out almost daily. Chris was teaching composition at the Ramblerny School for the Performing Arts in New Hope, and in the city he had organized the New York Improvisational

CHRIS AND I HAD MET THE summer after he was graduated from Dartmouth College with a pre-med degree. He abandoned medicine and went to Berklee College of Music in Boston, then toured the United States and the United Kingdom with Stan Kenton's band. He spent time in Mexico and went to South America on a State Department tour. Chris and Mike Gibbs were the first jazz composers ever accepted at Tanglewood Music School in the Berkshires where he studied with Aaron Copland, Gunther Schüller, and Yannis Xenakis.

Ensemble (NYIE). Chris and my brother Thomas, a photographer, featured the NYIE in a short movie they made called *Tue. Afternoon*. It was entered in the Edinburgh Film Festival, won a prize, and was shown on PBS several times as part of their "Film Generation" series. I appeared in one of the shots, just barely, far in the background . . . knitting. I often went into the city with Chris, and I sold a number of sweater designs to Spinnerin, which were then published in *McCall's* and *Vogue* magazines. I received my first designer byline for four sweaters that appeared in an issue of *Woman's Day* magazine.

In the thick of the Vietnam war, Chan and Phil moved their family to France (where Chan lives to this day—we remain very close friends), and we moved, with our new baby Cully, to the small village of Trumansburg in the Finger Lakes region of upstate New York. There Chris became the composer-in-residence for Bob Moog's fledgling synthesizer company and he built a studio onto our old 1836 house.

We became part of the Trumansburg community, and one winter in early December we organized a weekend Craft Sale in Moog's barn. The huge attendance startled us and I remember rushing home in the middle of the first morning to knit like ters, painters, and auto mechanics; the resulting paintings, cups, and bowls remain cherished items to this day; the VW bugs are long gone.

While in Trumansburg, I oozed into the mail-order business with my mother; she called me her Branch in the East. When our family of four eventually moved to Cary Bluff in central Wisconsin, Elizabeth and I were in daily contact and we became a designing and writing team in earnest. There was a brief five-month stay in Los Angeles when Chris was commissioned to write a suite for The Orchestra which was performed at the Dorothy Chandler Pavilion. His intense, creative activity permeated our apartment, and I churned out actual fashion knitting for shops during the pervasive waist-length-couturier-sweater period of that year. The kids were either knitting, decorating their homework, or tootling on wooden recorders issued by their Waldorf School, Highland Hall. Liesl's fifth-grade class was making k1, p1 ribbed socks on five #2 double-pointed needles, and Cully's class was knitting dolls, also on fine sets of double-pointed needles. Although I had taught them the rudiments of knitting, in a way our children learned to knit at school.

mad, as all of my woolly hats had been sold. I hear that the Craft Sale, still extant, has become a veritable institution. During the years in upstate New York, I knitted a number of barter-sweaters for pot-

Elizabeth and Gaffer (Arnold) reading each other's books.

Knitting Camp 1990. The "Afghan for Elizabeth" was knitted by the campers for her 80th birthday.

Elizabeth was invited to teach at the country's first knitting retreat in 1974 at a University of Wisconsin extension. The campus is on Shell Lake, and the word spread rather quickly among Elizabeth's followers. We all went the following year, and while Elizabeth and I were in class, my father (Gaffer), Chris, and the kids would sail, swim, and fish. Two knitters have been attending longer than I have: Lois Young and Jean Krebs. To date neither has missed a summer. We're heading into our twenty-sixth year as I write this and our

WE RETURNED TO LA A FEW YEARS LATER to attend the Grammy awards ceremony. Chris received a nomination for his album with Phil Woods: *Piper at the Gates of Dawn*.

Knitting Camp has expanded from one session to four. We are no longer scrunched into University student housing, which is how Camp originally got its name, but have shifted to a comparatively palatial convention motel in central Wisconsin.

Chris and I backed into the publishing business when Elizabeth could not find a taker for her third book and video series. So we did it ourselves (with rented video equipment and electric typewriter), and her fourth book/video as well (with our own computer and video stuff). At present we have published nineteen books, produced sixteen instructional videos, and I just mailed out Wool Gathering #60. The cross-country workshop tours and knitting videos ceased when Chris died in December, 1995, but the books, Wool Gathering, mail-order business (because of my assistant, Eleanor Haase), Knitting Camps (because of Eleanor, Amy Detjen,

Cristie Finbraaten, and Nancy Robinson) and magazine articles continue. And now this book.

Since I can assume that anyone reading these words is a knitter, it is really not necessary for me to describe or explain the importance of knitting in all aspects of my life. Suffice it to say I am exceedingly grateful to have an unending passion for something so creatively expressive, comfortingly soothing, mysteriously beautiful, and eminently practical. And one of the best parts is that knitting is a living, breathing thing—exciting, regenerating, and continuously evolving.

Scores of knitters around the world will nod their heads in agreement when I say that nearly everything I know about knitting I learned from Elizabeth Zimmermann. All the techniques and "unventions" of hers are wonderful, but perhaps her best lessons are philosophical ones. She was never pedantic about it, but embedded in her prose and knitting instructions is a persistent message of encouragement, self-empowerment, and pleasure. She has a great sense of humor combined with an irreverence for rules—both in knitting and in life. Thanks, Ma.

Instructional videos were made to accompany a number of the designs included in this book—they are listed on page 143. The tapes were made during what Chris and I called Knitting Vacations: We packed up knitting supplies and video and painting equipment and headed out with a rough plan for a garment. As the design progressed, Chris taped each interesting point in real time. Only occasionally did we have a finished garment to hold up in advance to show where we were going. Chris was uniquely qualified for the job of videographer (he was also the editor, plus he wrote and performed

Chris and me, 1985.

the music for each tape) as his mental knitting skills were equal to, and often surpassed, my own. As the videographer, he not only dealt with the lighting, framing, zooming, and focus, but actually listened to what I was saying; correcting me when I spoke in error or reminding me when I omitted something. He even invented a new knitting technique on the air (*Camera Guy's I-Cord Variation* for the Round-the-Bend Jacket, which appears in the *Handknitting with Meg Swansen* book and video.) For over three decades I never plotted a design without Chris's input. I am unable to summon the words to impart the importance of my husband to my life. He was my business partner as well as my life partner, and the depth to which I miss him is indescribable.

Tools, Techniques, and Terms

The following is a list of techniques I used while making the garments in this book. Most of the methods suggested are just that—suggestions. You may use whatever techniques you like, but consider experimenting with alternative methods that may prove useful for future projects.

Tools

Here is a list of basic tools. I have not listed these items for each garment.

Scissors

Needle gauge

Stitch holders or odd lengths of wool for stitch holders

Large-eyed *sharp* needle for darning in ends

Large-eyed *blunt* needle for weaving, duplicate stitch, or sewing a seam

Magnetic row finder for keeping your place when following a pattern chart

Coil-less pin markers: These are safety pins that do not have the little coil at the base which may get tangled in your stitches. Another advantage of this type of marker is that you can place it directly into the important stitch. I prefer them to ring markers, which have to be moved every row/round and are liable to fall off and roll under the sofa.

Techniques and Terms

Balance stitches To balance a color pattern on a drop-shoulder cardigan, I begin at the center back and mirror-image each side of each armhole cutting-stitch as follows: Mark the armhole cutting-stitches. Count the remaining stitches across the back of the body between markers and locate the center-back stitch(es). Beginning at the center-back stitch, count in increments of the pattern repeat to the armhole (not counting the cutting stitches), noting which stitch in the pattern repeat you end on. Begin with the same stitch on the other side of the armhole and count in increments of the pattern repeat to the center front. This will give you the "starting stitch" for your pattern. The starting stitch should also be the "ending stitch" at the end of the round. Fudge a stitch or two if necessary to insure an exact balance each side of the center front.

Casting on

Backward loop cast-on Make a loop in the yarn and place it on the needle backward so that it doesn't unwind. Repeat for desired number of stitches, adjusting tension as needed.

Cable cast-on Also sometimes called "knitted-on" cast-on. To eliminate the need for a knot, cast on two stitches using the long-tail method (see page 14). *Insert tip of right needle between the two stitches (figure 1), yarn over the needle and pull a loop of working wool through (figure 2), put loop on left needle (figure 3). Repeat from *.

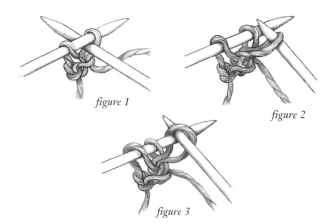

figure 1

figure 2

figure 3

German twisted cast-on This type of long-tail cast-on provides more elasticity than the regular version. I also recommend it to prevent corrugated ribbing from curling.

Set up as for the long-tail cast-on (see page 14). Take the needle under both of the thumb strands. Coming toward yourself (over the far thumb strand), insert the needle down into the center of the thumb loop and bring the needle toward you (figure 1). The loop around your thumb will have a twist in it, close to the needle (figure 2). Complete as for long-tail method, turning your thumb slightly to remove the twist in the loop and allowing the needle to pass through the untwisted loop (figures 3 and 4).

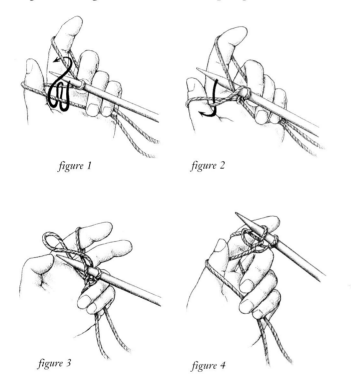

figure 1   *figure 2*

figure 3   *figure 4*

Invisible cast-on Also called "provisional method." I use the "twisty wrap" method (below), but the crochet-chain method may be easier to understand.

Twisty-wrap This method is worked with two yarns; the working yarn and a contrasting waste yarn. Place a loose slip knot of working yarn on the needle. Hold the waste yarn next to the slip knot and wind the working yarn under the waste yarn, over the needle, and in front of and then behind the waste yarn for the desired number of stitches. When you're ready to work in the opposite direc-

tion, remove the waste yarn and pick up the raw stitches.

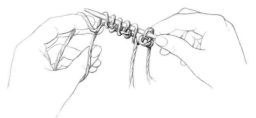

Crochet chain With a crochet hook, make a loose chain of waste yarn about six or eight stitches more than you need to cast on. Two threads form a V on the front of the chain, and a third thread on the back forms loops. Knit up stitches through the back loops (figure 1). Do not pull the waste yarn out until you are ready to pick up the loops to knit them (figure 2). As a time and motion freak, I loved Medrith Glover's tip to crochet right over the needle. Chain a few links. Hold the chain and needle in your left hand. With crochet hook in your right hand, *loop the working wool over the needle from front to back. Chain another link. Repeat from *. Isn't that neat?

figure 1   *figure 2*

Knitted cast-on This one is similar to the cable cast-on (see page 12), but the right needle goes *into* the first stitch on the left needle rather than between two stitches. *Insert tip of right needle into stitch on left needle, yarn over needle and pull a loop of working wool through as if to knit (figure 1), and put this loop on left needle (figure 2). Repeat from *.

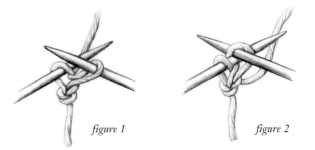

figure 1   *figure 2*

Long-tail cast-on This is the most widely used type of cast-on. Leaving a long tail, place thumb and index finger of your left hand between the two strands and secure the long ends with your other three fingers. Spread your thumb and index finger. Aim the needle down into the space between the thumb-forefinger yarn and your hand. Point the needle to the ceiling. That twist is your first "free" stitch (figure 1). Now pull the needle down and you will see a loop form in front of your left thumb. Put the needle up into that loop from below (figure 2). Hook the near-forefinger strand down through the loop (figure 3). Release your left thumb (figure 4). As you reset your thumb, the stitch will snug onto the needle.

Casting off

Regular old cast-off Knit one stitch, *knit one stitch, pass the first stitch over the second and off the needle. Rep from * until one stitch remains, pull yarn through last stitch to secure.

2-stitch I-cord cast-off Make two backward loops (cord stitches) on the end of the left needle, which holds the stitches to be cast off. *Knit one stitch, knit the last cord stitch together with the stitch to be cast off through their back loops (figures 1 and 2), replace these two stitches onto the left needle (figure 3), and repeat from *. (*For fussy knitters* [FFK]: Return one stitch to left needle, leave next stitch on right needle, insert tip of left needle into front of this stitch and knit. Yes, this results in a twisted stitch, but it is very tidy looking, and you can zip along at great speed.)

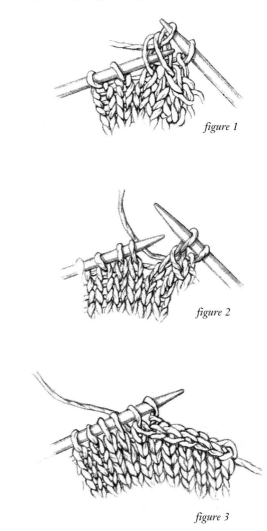

figure 1

figure 2

figure 3

2-stitch I-cord cast-off

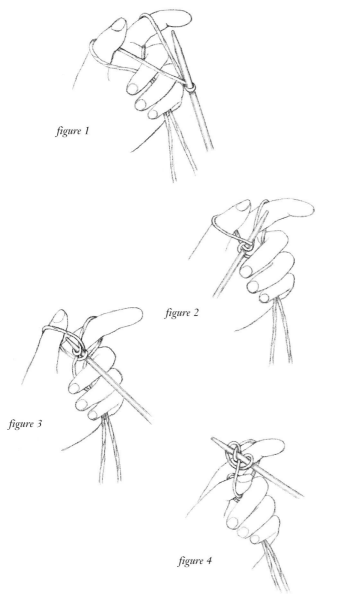

figure 1

figure 2

figure 3

figure 4

Long-tail cast-on

3-needle, 2-stitch I-cord cast-off Hold the two needles with stitches to be joined parallel with insides facing. Onto a third needle, cast on two I-cord stitches and transfer them to one of the parallel needles. Working firmly, *knit the first cord stitch, slip the second cord stitch, knit together one stitch each from the front and back needle, and pass the slipped stitch over the last stitch made. Replace the two cord stitches to one of the parallel needles and rep from * until two cord stitches remain. Break wool, thread it through the two cord stitches. Darn in end. (See also Joyce's variation on page 18.)

EZ's sewn method (or sewn cast-off) This is an exceedingly elastic cast-off and is particularly handsome on garter stitch. Thread working wool through a blunt needle. Working from right to left,

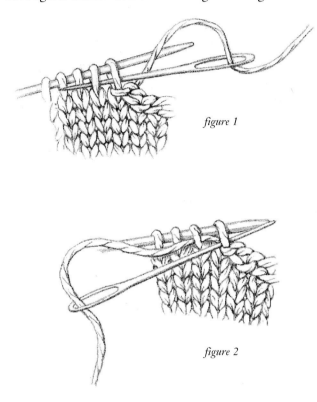

figure 1

figure 2

*put needle through first two stitches (figure 1). Put needle back through first stitch from left to right (figure 2) and slip it off left needle. Repeat from *.

Corrugated ribbing This two-color ribbing is worked with one color for the knit stitches and the other for the purl stitches. This ribbing has very little elasticity but nice stability. The weight matches that of an allover color-patterned garment. To

prevent curling, use the German twisted cast-on (see page 13).

Double-decrease There are several ways of turning three stitches into one, but my favorite is this. Slip two stitches together knitwise, slip one stitch purlwise, place the left needle into the fronts of the three slipped stitches and knit them together through back loops.

DFD (dreaded frontal droop) This is when cardigan bands droop below the rest of the lower edge.

Duplicate stitch Also called Swiss embroidery, this stitch essentially duplicates an existing knitted stitch with yarn on a sewing needle.

Horizontal Bring the threaded needle out from back to front at the base of the V of the knitted stitch you want to cover. *Working right to left, pass needle in and out under the stitch in the row above it and back into the base of the same stitch. Bring the needle back out at the base of the V of the next stitch to the left. Repeat from *.

Vertical Beginning at lowest point, work as for horizontal duplicate stitch, ending by bringing the needle back out at the base of the stitch directly above the stitch just worked.

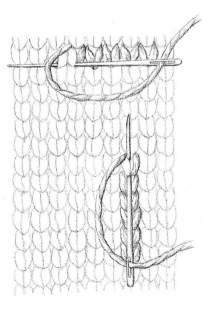

EPS (Elizabeth's percentage system) Elizabeth Zimmermann's percentage system enables you to custom design a garment according to your personal gauge. This system is ideal for knitters who want to make the best use of a handspun wool, which seeks its own gauge.

After knitting several swatches, choose the one you like best and determine the gauge. Multiply the number of stitches per inch by the number of inches you want the garment to be at the widest point (usually just below the armholes). That answer is [K], the "key number", or 100%. Other calculations will be a percentage of [K]. For instance, the lower ribbing may be 90% of [K]; the cuff will be 20 to 25% of [K]; yoke-style sleeves will be increased to 35 to 40% of [K]; drop-shoulder sleeves will increase to 40 to 50% of [K]. Depending on the style of garment, these guidelines may be honed by your personal preference and the size and shape idiosyncrasies of the recipient.

Half-weave This is a method of uniting raw stitches with an existing fabric or selvedge. The raw stitches are treated as you would for Kitchener stitch (see page 19), but just sewn (in and out) to the opposing fabric.

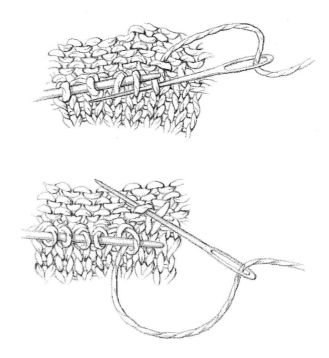

Hems

Afterthought hem I recommend that you neither cast on nor cast off a hem. Both techniques (with exceptions, of course) cause a tight, unyielding selvedge that when sewn or knitted to the inside of the sweater will not stretch with the rest of the fabric, causing an unfortunate horizontal demarcation. So, unless you use an invisible (or provisional) cast-on (see page 13), do not think about the hem until after you finish the sweater. In order for the afterthought hem to work, I encourage you to use the long-tail cast-on (see page 14) and to arrange matters so that the outline-stitch side is *outside* and the purl bumps are *inside* (see page 17). Knit on. When you've completed the garment, come back to the original cast-on and, with a lighter weight wool (to obviate bulk), knit up into the purl bumps of the cast-on stitches, one stitch for every cast-on stitch (figure 1). The outline stitch forms a nice, sharp fold line. Knit the hem to desired depth, incorporating a secret message, or the wearer's name and the date, the name of the sweater, a private joke, or

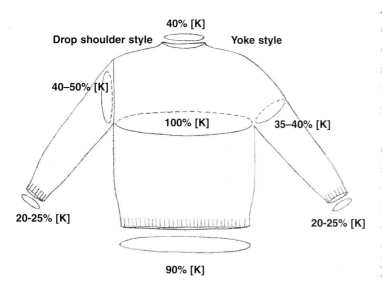

Drop shoulder style — Yoke style

40% [K]

40–50% [K]

100% [K]

35–40% [K]

20-25% [K]   20-25% [K]

90% [K]

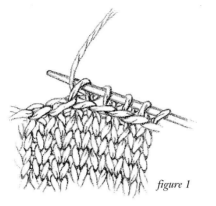

figure 1

continue knitting. *When you arrive back at center front, slide the wrapped yarn off the needle and rewrap another nine times (figure 1). Continue from * until hem is desired depth. Cut through the wraps (figure 2), sew the hem into place, and tuck the wrap-ends into the hem tube before tacking the vertical edges together.

If you have old sweaters with flaring hems—knitted before you knew all these tricks—run a gentle elastic through the tube.

perhaps a pretty pattern. One of our customers made a sweater for her son and into the hem knitted "Tidy Your Room."

When done, do not cast off, but sew the raw stitches down with a sharp needle by lightly skimming through the back of the body and through the raw stitch. Stay in a straight horizontal line (figure 2). Now the hem will breathe with the rest of the

figure 1

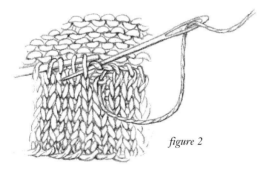

figure 2

fabric. If you cannot come up with a lighter weight wool for the hem, knit one round on all stitches then reduce the number by 10% (k8, k2tog). This will help to hold the hem in. And for a super neat job, if the hem is in a contrasting color, knit the last round or two in the matching color of the round to which it will be sewn.

Cardigan hem To put a hem onto a cardigan and maintain a neat front edge, stitch and cut the body open *before* you knit the hem. Then knit up all stitches around lower edge as described above. Install a "wrapped steek" as follows: At center front, wrap the yarn(s) around the needle nine times and

figure 2

I-cord This is a tube made of circular stocking stitch. For 3-stitch I-cord, cast on three stitches on a double-pointed needle. *Knit three stitches, slide them to the other end of the needle and repeat from *.

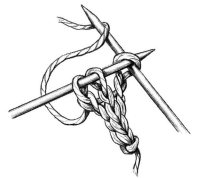

4-sided, 3-stitch I-cord Work as above but instead of knitting all three stitches, work them as knit one, purl one, knit one.

Double I-cord This is simply a second applied I-cord attached to an existing I-cord.

Elizabeth's applied I-cord This border is knitted directly onto picked-up stitches of a selvedge. For 3-stitch I-cord, *knit two cord stitches, knit the third cord stitch together with one picked-up stitch through their back loops (or slip third st, K one picked-up st, psso.) Repeat from *. The cord may be two, three, or four stitches wide.

Elizabeth's built-in I-cord For stocking-stitch tube selvedges on garter stitch. *Knit to last two (or three) stitches. With wool forward, slip two (or three) stitches purwise. Turn. Repeat from *.

Elizabeth's hidden I-cord buttonholes Work Elizabeth's applied I-cord onto a selvedge. When you get to a place you'd like to put a buttonhole, work three rounds of I-cord without applying it, slide three picked-up stitches off the left needle, then resume applying to the edge. Vary the number of unattached rounds to get desired buttonhole size.

Empirical method for I-cord Apply a few inches of cord and take a look to see if it gives the results you want. If it is too loose or too tight, make necessary adjustments.

Looped I-cord buttonholes Work Elizabeth's applied I-cord onto a selvedge. When you get to a place you'd like to put a buttonhole, work eight or nine rounds of I-cord without applying, then resume applying to the edge, forming a loop. Vary the number of unattached rounds to get desired buttonhole size.

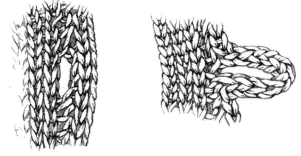

hidden I-cord buttonhole *looped I-cord buttonhole*

Joyce Williams's CC I-cord method Because applying I-cord in a strongly contrasting color causes blips of the previous color to show through on the side that faces you as you work, I used to apply the cord to the "wrong" side of the garment and not worry about the blips. But now, thanks to designer Joyce Williams, we can defeat the blip as follows. For a 3-stitch I-cord, *Knit two stitches, slip one stitch, yarnover (figure 1), knit one picked-up stitch (figure 2), pass the slipped stitch and the yarnover over the last stitch (figure 3). Repeat from *.

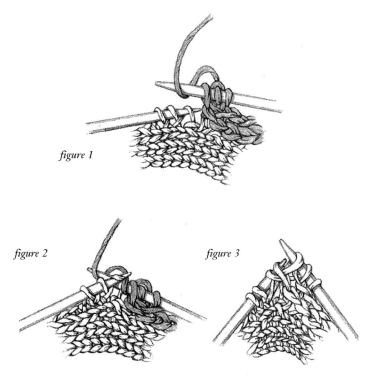

figure 1

figure 2   *figure 3*

Jogless circular color pattern Circular knitting progresses in a spiral, and the end of a round never exactly meets the beginning. To obviate the "jog" that usually occurs, you need to keep the beginning of the round from travelling through a motif. (If you're working an interlocking allover motif, there is little you can do beyond judiciously darning in the beginning and end of the color-motif yarn ends.) If the motifs are not connected, as for a heart, for instance, you can mentally reassign the first stitch of the round and always finish knitting horizontally through the last heart motif before moving up to the next round. The "first" stitch of the round will veer to the left or right up the diagonal of the side of the heart.

When you're working solid-color stripes of two or more rounds, *at the end of the first round of the new color, pick up the right side of the stitch in the row below (it will be the old color), put it on the left needle and k2tog. This will move the first stitch of the round one stitch to the left. Move your marker accordingly and continue the stripe for the wanted number of rounds. Repeat from * for each color change.

Kangaroo pouch This is the funny shape formed when a largish number of underarm or neck stitches are put on a piece of wool and a few steek stitches are cast on in their place.

Kitchener stitch This is also called grafting and is used to weave raw stitches together. Bring a blunt threaded needle through the front stitch as if to purl and leave the stitch on the needle. Bring threaded needle through the back stitch as if to knit and leave the stitch on the needle. *Bring threaded needle

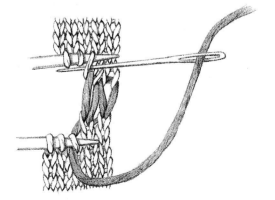

through the same front stitch as if to knit and slip this stitch off the needle. Bring the threaded needle through the next front stitch as if to purl and leave the stitch on the needle. Bring threaded needle through the first back stitch as if to purl, slip that stitch off, and then bring the needle through the next back stitch as if to knit and leave this stitch on the needle. Repeat from * until no stitches remain.

Knit up Hook the working wool through the selvedge stitches (as opposed to pick up, which is done without any working wool). Knit the stitch through the back loop.

Knit-up ratio When you're knitting a garter-stitch border onto a stocking-stitch body, knit up a ratio of two stitches for every three rounds and the garter stitch will lie flat. When applying I-cord, the knit-up ratio is not so precise, and you must experiment to see what will work best.

Knitting back backwards (KBB) This is not a parlor trick, but a most useful technique. It is actually purling back from the "right" side. *Put the left needle into the back of the stitch on the right needle. Wrap the wool over the top of the left needle and around from front to back, pull a loop through and slide the stitch off the right needle. Repeat from *.

Knitting into the back of the stitch of the row below This is the most invisible increase that I know of. With the tip of the right needle, pick up (from behind) the right side of the next stitch in the row below (figure 1). Insert the tip of the left needle into the front of this stitch and complete the stitch by knitting it through the back loop (figure 2). Then work the stitch on the needle as usual. The result is a twisted stitch that is tucked behind the parent stitch in a nearly invisible manner. To make a mirror image, knit the parent stitch first, then with the left needle pick up the left side of the stitch from the row below and knit into the front of it.

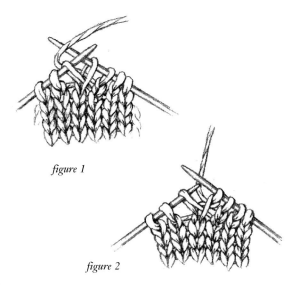

figure 1

figure 2

Knitting with two circular needles This is Joyce Williams's invention to eliminate double-pointed needles. (She knits glove fingers on two 24" circulars.) Have half the total stitches on each circular. Knit with the beginning and end of one needle. When you've knitted all stitches, pull the needle out a bit and pick up the beginning and end of the second needle. Knit those stitches—one round is complete. You need only change needles twice per round instead of three or four times as with double-pointed needles.

Machine stitching and cutting With a blunt sewing needle and contrasting color, baste down the center of your steek. Using a small stitch and loose tension, machine stitch down one side of the basting, across the bottom, and up the other side. If this is your first time cutting, add a second, reassuring line of stitching on top of the first. Stay as close to the center basting as possible—yea, even unto stitching into the right and left halves of the center stitch itself (which is my preferred method). Cut between the stitching lines.

Magnetic row finder For ease in following pattern charts, I highly recommend a Magnetic row finder. It consists of an 8 × 11" (20.5 × 28 cm) metal board

and three magnet strips. Place a photocopy of the pattern chart on the board and snap a magnet strip over the line just above the one you are reading. (If you put it below the line, it obliterates what you have just knitted and prevents you from double-checking your accuracy that *this* stitch belongs above *that* stitch.) The Magnetic row finder is invaluable for following intricate color or texture pattern charts.

Mitered corners
Inward miter Work a double-decrease over the three corner stitches every other row. My favorite double-decrease is to slip two stitches together knitwise, slip the next stitch purlwise, place the left needle into the fronts of the slipped stitches and knit them together through their back loops.

Outward miter Increase one stitch each side of corner stitch every other row.

One-row buttonholes (Elizabeth Zimmermann's method)
Slip one stitch purlwise. Bring wool forward (figure 1). Slip one stitch purlwise. Pass first slipped stitch over second (figure 2).

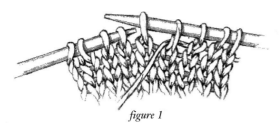

figure 1

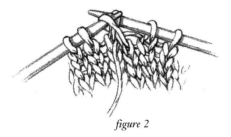

figure 2

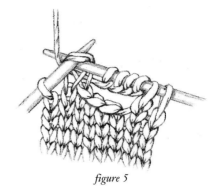

figure 5

Slip one stitch purlwise. Pass second slipped stitch over third. Slip one stitch purlwise. Pass third slipped stitch over fourth. Put fourth stitch on left needle, reversing it. Reverse (twist or turn) stitch on right needle (figure 3). Pull wool firmly, lay it over

Outline stitch of long-tail cast-on The long-tail cast-on (see page 14) yields a different appearance on either side. One side looks like the outline stitch in embroidery (figure 1); the other side looks like purl bumps (figure 2). In order to provide the sharp turn for a hem, assign the outline stitch to the "right" side.

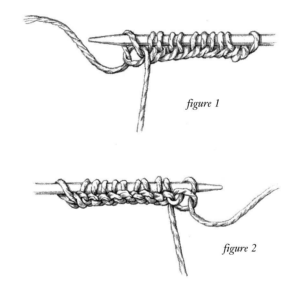

figure 1

figure 2

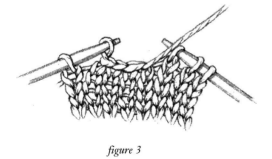

figure 3

right needle from front to back, and pass turned stitch over it (figure 4). Make four backward loops (see page 12) over right needle and knit two stitches together (figure 5).

Peeries This is a Scottish term for the small bands of color pattern between the larger OXOs of Fair Isle knitting.

Phony seam This is a demarcation to detail the side "seam" of a garment body or sleeve; it may be used decoratively. This technique makes it easy to locate the exact seam lines when you're blocking a sweater or cutting for an armhole. When you flop down the damp garment, you needn't "find" the seam stitches. The body and sleeves will automatically fold at the exact seam lines.

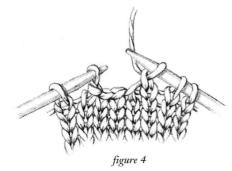

figure 4

For stocking stitch Drop a stitch off the needle and let it down to desired point. With a crochet hook, *hook up two ladders together (figure 1), then one. Repeat from * to the top. That single, vertical line will have one-third fewer rows than the rest of the piece and will form a welt (figure 2). Use this technique on the body and sleeves.

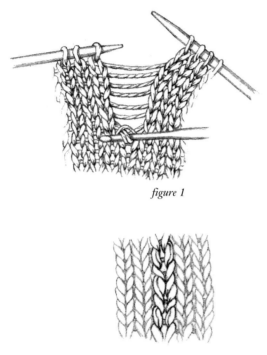

figure 1

figure 2

For garter stitch Drop a stitch off the needle and let it down to desired point. With a crochet hook, hook up two ladders at a time.

For reversible garter stitch Drop a stitch off the needle and let it down to desired point. See how the garter stitch separates into front and back ladders? (You can put your finger down between them.) Grab the dropped stitch and hook up each front stitch (in reality, every other row). Then, because you have already used the dropped stitch, twist a loose strand of wool into a stitch on the other side and hook up every remaining ladder.

Purl when you can (PWYC) Use this method to prevent curling when you want to begin a garment with a color pattern instead of a standard lower-edge treatment. When you purl a white stitch into a black stitch, it pulls black up into the white row and makes a blip. This is a beautiful design feature in Bohus knitting but, in my opinion, should be used judiciously in other areas. If the stitch is white and above a white stitch or a black above a black stitch, it can be purled. A black stitch above a white stitch or vice versa, should be knitted. I usually choose only one color to purl, either the pattern or backgound color.

Sew down the raw stitches of a hem With a sharp needle, skim through the back of the body, then through a raw stitch.

Short rows and wrapping This technique inserts extra rows in the middle of the fabric in either flat or circular knitting. It may be used to lengthen the back of the body to prevent "riding up" and/or to raise and shape the shoulders. Knit to the turning point. *Slip the next stitch to right needle (figure 1). Bring wool to the front and replace slipped stitch onto left needle (figure 2). Turn. See? The working wool has been wrapped around the base of the slipped stitch. Work to the other end of the short row (figure 3; or do not turn and KBB; see page 19). Repeat from *. Work to first wrap, then knit the wrap together with the slipped stitch.

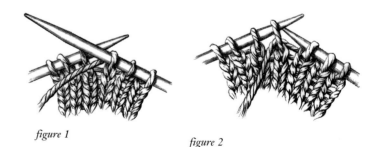

figure 1

figure 2

figure 3

Sleeves

Knitted in If you'd rather knit than sew, do not cast off the sleeve top. Knit up a corresponding number of stitches around the armhole. Hold the two needles parallel to each other with insides together. With a third needle, work 3-needle cast-off as follows: Knit together one stitch from each needle. *Knit together the next stitch from each needle, pass the first stitch over the last. Repeat from *. You may add a 2- or 3-stitch I-cord for a more obvious bead around the armhole.

Sewn in Pin the center sleeve top to the shoulder seam and pin the underarm to the bottom of the armhole opening. Pin the halfway points, then the quarter-way points. Sew the sleeve in from the "right" side, never veering from your chosen vertical sewing line on the body. Because the stitches and rows do not match up in plain stocking stitch, do not bother counting them—simply dive in and out with the tapestry needle on the sleeve, then on the body, with the pins guiding the relationship of sleeve stitches to body rounds.

Splicing (for wool only) Untwist the plies of both new and old ends for about 4 to 5" (10 to 12.5 cm). Break (do not cut) off one-half of the plies from each end (figure 1). Line up the remaining ends so that the broken parts overlap slightly on your left palm (figure 2). Wet your right palm. Rub the overlapped ends tog swiftly for five seconds. The combination of heat and moisture will fuse the ends with no noticeable thickening (figure 3). Make the breaks long enough so that at least two to three stitches can be knitted with the overlapped section.

figure 1

figure 2

figure 3

Steek This a term for the extra stitches that are cast on and later cut when a garment is knitted entirely in the round. The extra stitches are worked at the center front, armholes, and neck.

Crocheted steek This machineless technique was originated by Mary Hounsell at Knitting Camp a few years ago, and is being refined by Katherine Pence, Joyce Williams, and Amy Detjen as I write this. I used it on the Weeping Sun, Celtic Swirl, and Phoenix.

For a two-colored garment, when you cast on the steek stitches for an armhole, *do not* use the backward loop method (see page 12), but rather the long-tail method (see page 14) with both strands of working wool. If you're working a solid-color garment, use the cable method to cast on. You need cast on only three stitches, but you may want to use five if this is your first venture. Be sure to keep the steek stitches in alternate color speckles throughout. When you've finished the body, work a crochet chain for a few stitches, then secure the chain to the cast-on stitches. Continue up the steek by working a crochet chain as follows.

Think of the three stitches as six halves: a left and right side of each of stitches 1, 2, and 3. You want to crochet together the right side of stitch 1 with the left side of stitch 2. Work up one side of the steek (figures 1 and 2). Loop about a dozen chains in the

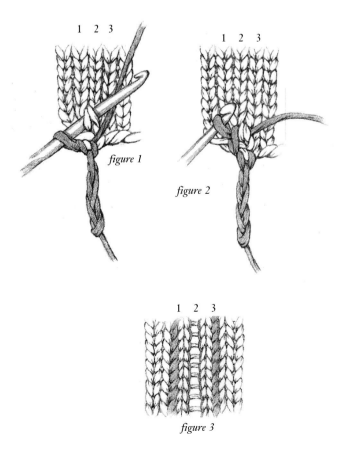

figure 1

figure 2

figure 3

air and then come down the other side, connecting the right side of stitch 2 with the left side of stitch 3. End by securing the chain to the cast-on stitches. As you look between the chains you will see only the horizontal bars in the center of the middle stitches (figure 3). Cut through the bars, being careful not to snip the crochet. There you are. No machine stitching necessary.

Ladder steek This type of steek is similar to the wrapped steek used on a cardigan hem (see page 17), but is formed by raveling existing stitches rather than wrapping the working wool around the needle every round.

Wrapped steek (See Cardigan hem, page 17.)

Washing and Blocking I usually block a sweater before I sew on the buttons or finish the cut edges, letting the garment settle in to where it intends to remain. First, try the thing on (or have the recipient try it on) and make notes of any areas you wish to alter: Do you want another 1" (2.5 cm) of sleeve or body length? Is the body a tad too narrow or too wide? Subtle adjustments such as these may be made during the blocking of wool garments.

Add a capful of pure, liquid soap to a sink full of cool water. Submerge the garment and let it soak for a few minutes. Squish it gently, then squeeze out all excess water. Rinse several times in matching-temperature water, squeeze, and take it to the washing machine. Run it through the spin-cycle only for about a minute (or wrap it in a bath towel and jump on it, or swing it around your head in a salad basket). At this stage, the damp garment is totally malleable. As you lay it flat, the sleeves may be pulled to make them longer and narrower—or widened to make them shorter. The same goes for the body. Measure to make sure both sleeves are the same length and that the circumference is what you want. If you inserted short rows, the back will be just a bit longer than the front. Pull the mitered corners out nice and sharp, and yank the ribbed cuffs long and narrow. Depending upon the weather, the garment should dry in a day; flip it over when partially dry. *Note:* Many mills have dif-

ficulty removing all the excess dye in dark shades. I occasionally find that black or dark green will flood the water during the first wash. But I've never known it to infect any other color in the sweater.

Abbreviations

beg	begin, beginning
CC	contrast color
CO	cast on
cont	continue, continuing
dbl	double
dec('d)	decrease(d), decreasing
fwd	forward
inc('d)	increase(d), increasing
k	knit
kwise	knitwise
k2tog	knit 2 together
M1	make one (increase 1 stitch)
MC	main color
p	purl
pwise	purlwise
p2so	pass 2 stitches over
p2sso	pass 2 slipped stitches over
rnd(s)	round(s)
RS	right side
sl	slip
ssk	slip 1, slip 1, knit the 2 slipped stitches together through back loops
st(s)	stitch(es)
tbl	through back loop(s)
tog	together
WS	wrong side
wyib	with yarn in back
wyif	with yarn in front
yo	yarnover

"Four-handed knitting." Ma and me knitting around on the same garment.

Introduction to the Patterns

BEING MY MOTHER'S DAUGHTER, I STRONGLY believe that every knitter is unique, that each of us has our own idiosyncratic method of applying our craft, and that there is no "wrong" way to knit. If you obtain the results you want, you are doing it "right". With that in mind, following stitch-for-stitch instructions can often result in disappointment—if you rely too heavily on the printed page, you may not be paying close enough attention to your actual knitting. Elizabeth Zimmermann taught a generation of knitters to *look at their knitting* and to trust what they see above what they read.

I believe that instructions for the basic construction and knowledge of your own personal gauge and EPS (Elizabeth's Percentage System) is all you need to knit a perfectly fitting garment. However, I know that many knitters are still gathering the confidence to plunge ahead on their own, so you will find specific instructions in several sizes for most of the garments. For accuracy of the sizes I have leaned heavily on the skill and cleverness of the editing team: Dorothy Ratigan, Judith Durant and Ann Budd.

I am pleased to present my designs for you to use as a starting point.

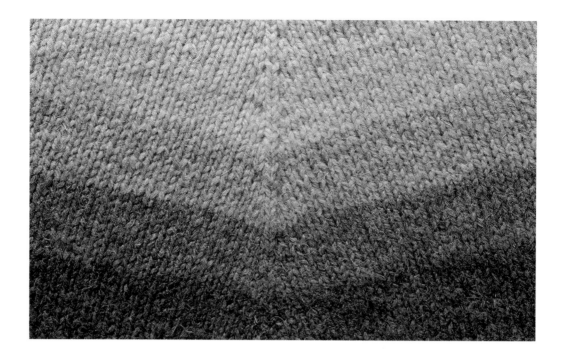

Box-the-Compass
Yoke Sweater

A WORD ABOUT SEAMLESS YOKE SWEATERS: THIS was a shape Elizabeth worked with for many decades. After knitting scores of them, she came up with a formula that Chris dubbed "Elizabeth's Percentage System," or EPS. The formula is based on the concept that in an average adult-sized sweater there is a mathematical relationship between the circumference of the body and the circumference of the cuff, upper sleeve, and neck. Basically, if the number of body stitches at the widest point is considered to be 100% (or key number, [K]), the number of stitches to cast on at the cuffs will be about 20–25% of the body stitches; you will increase the sleeve to about 35–40%. Sleeves and body are united at the underarm where 8% of the body stitches will go onto holders. The yoke stitches (100% + 35% + 35% minus 4 x 8%) are then decreased to 40% at the neck (or to 50% for children, who have proportionally larger heads).

Elizabeth also discovered that the depth of the yoke (by measurement) is approximately one-half the width of the body; Medrith Glover adds that yoke depth is rarely over 10" (25.5 cm) regardless of body girth. Naturally, these are only guidelines and the percentages will fluctuate as you custom fit your design to a specific shape.

Once the sleeves and body have been amalgamated onto one needle, it is then time to decide what style of sweater you want: yoke, raglan, saddle sleeve, shirt-yoke, hybrid, entrelac, sideways yoke, set-in sleeve, spoke yoke, lap-shoulder, spiral yoke, or box-the-compass; they all begin in an identical manner until the body and sleeves are joined.

The Box-the-Compass design is the result of a collaboration between Ma and me. We were hanging out one day, talking about knitting. Elizabeth wondered about rotating the four raglan shaping lines so they would appear at the center front and

back and on the sleeve tops. So confident was she (behind a nearly perfect track record) that she immediately cast on an adult-sized sweater and worked the yoke shaping as she had hypothesized. A few weeks later she brought the finished sweater for me to try on. What a hoot. The sleeves were lovely with the decreases running smoothly down the shoulder line; but the centers front and back stood out in sharp cone-shaped points. Even in the face of that physical evidence—so unused was she to being wrong—Elizabeth came up and patted me on the breastbone. "Oh, that'll block out," she said. Nuh-uh. As you probably know from shaping the top of a cap, if you suddenly begin a double decrease in the middle of a field of plain stocking stitch, you get a pronounced blip. So we cogitated and came up with the following scheme.

In Elizabeth's design for a circular set-in-sleeve sweater, 4 stitches are decreased *every* round until 40% of the body stitches remain at the neck. Then

there are the familiar 8 stitches decreased every *second* round for a raglan shape. Right. So why not 12 stitches every third round? 16 stitches every fourth round? 20 stitches every fifth round?

How about having the underarm phony seam on the *top* side of the sleeve where it will melt into the center stitch of the double decrease and obviate the blip?

Aha. Let's also have two (or three) phony seams on the body fore and aft so that all 6 (or 8) can merge into the double decreases.

With those concepts in mind, we made several versions. The two shown here have 8 double-decrease points (16 sts) worked every 4th round.

Finished size

38 (40, 43)" (96.5 [101.5, 109] cm) bust/chest circumference; as long as you like. Yoke about 8½ (9, 10)" (21.5 [23, 25] cm) deep.

Yarn

Canadian Regal (100% wool; 272 yd/ 4 oz): MC, 4 (4, 5) skeins; CC, 1 skein each. Or Brown Sheep wool (190 yd/4 oz): MC 6 (6, 7) skeins; CC, 1 skein each.

Needles

Approximately size 5 (3.75 mm): 16" (40-cm) and 24" (60-cm) circular and set of double-pointed for lower sleeve.

Gauge

20 sts and 30 rnds = 4" (10 cm); 5 sts and 7½ rnds = 1" (2.5 cm).

Using Elizabeth's Percentage System (see page 16), multiply *your* gauge by desired circumference at widest part of body. The resulting number is the key number, or [K]—190 (200, 216) sts. Alter for symmetry.

For a ribbed or garter-st border, cast on 10% fewer than [K] sts. Inc to [K] in the first stocking-st rnd. The hemmed versions shown here have 5%

fewer sts cast on; the additional sts are increased gradually at the side "seams" about 4" (10 cm) apart vertically.

Body: With longer needle and using the long-tail method (see page 14), cast on [K]–5%—178 (188, 204) sts. Mark the diametrically opposed side sts. You may notice a slight discrepancy in the 5% reduction. Remember, as you inc at the side "seams" you are working in units of 4 sts per inc, so calculate accordingly.

Join, being careful not to twist sts. Work to desired length to underarm, inc 3 times, about 3 to 4" (7.5 to 10 cm) apart, which should bring you up to [K].

Note: On your way to the underarm you may want to work short rows to prevent the back from riding up (see "Short rows and wrapping" page 22).

Drop the exact underarm "seam" st down to the lower edge. With a crochet hook, hook it up again at a rate of 2 sts for every 3 rnds to make a phony seam (see page 21).

Place about 8% of [K] sts on holders at each underarm—15 (17, 17) sts. If necessary, alter by 1 st so that an uneven number of sts enables you to have a centered phony seam.

Sleeves: (hemmed) With double-pointed needles, cast on 20% of [K]—38 (40, 42) sts. Join, being careful not to twist sts. Work around for about 1" (2.5 cm). Mark 3 center underarm sts with a coil-less pin and inc 1 st each side of marked sts every 5th rnd. You may choose to make the incs in opposing directions . . . an optional bit of fussiness.

When the number of sts warrants, change to a 16" (40-cm) circular needle. Keep inc until you have about 37 (38, 40)% of [K]—70 (76, 86) sts. Then stop inc and work straight to desired length to underarm—18 to 20" (46 to 51 cm) for an average adult. Place about 8% of [K]—15 (17, 17) sts—on holders at each underarm, centered over the inc line. Drop the center underarm st and the exact opposite st at the top of the sleeve. Hook it up again as described above.

With underarms aligned, knit the sleeves onto the body, leaving all underarm sts on holders to be woven tog later. Work around on all sts for a few rnds. ***Shape back neck:*** Knit around all left sleeve sts plus 12 sts past sleeve/body join. Wrap the next st (see "Short rows and wrapping" page 22), turn, and work back to the same point past the right sleeve/body join. Wrap the next st and turn. *Work to 12 sts shy of last wrap and wrap again. Rep from * 3 more times (a total of 3 sets of short rows). Knit around on all sts, working the wraps tog with their slipped sts.

Yoke: You have a giant swatch—the body—from which to obtain an accurate row gauge. I get 7.5 rows per inch and I want the yoke to be 8½ (9, 10)" (21.5 [23, 25.5] cm) deep, which means I have about 62 (70, 75) rows in which to reduce 270 (292, 328) sts (sleeve and body sts minus underarm sts) to 76 (80, 86) sts at the neck (40% of [K]). With 8 dec points I will be getting rid of 16 sts every 4th rnd. Working 13 (13, 15) dec rnds will consume 208 (208, 240) sts, leaving 62 (76, 88) sts for the neck. Close enough.

Now then, 13 (13, 15) dec rnds × 4 (a dec every 4th rnd) = 52 (52, 60) rnds used up. With 62 (67, 75) rnds total height, that leaves 10 (15, 15) rnds plain before the first dec. If you worked a few rnds before the back-of-neck shaping, plus 6 shaping short rows, you already have most of the plain bit done and can begin dec in a few more rnds.

If the above sounds like gibberish, I will not be surprised; it will make much more sense when you are actually at that point on your sweater.

Before you begin to dec (using the 2 already-established sleeve-top lines as guides), divide both front and back yoke sts into 3 equidistant sections and work phony seams at each point. Place a coilless pin in each of the 8 phony seam sts and work a double dec (see page 15) at those points every 4th rnd as follows: *Work to 1 st before marker, sl 2tog kwise, k1, p2sso; rep from *. ***Stripes:*** Plan what colors you want for the yoke; you can shade from dark to light or vice versa; they can be equal or random widths. I began each new color behind the left shoulder where it would be the least noticeable, employing the jogless color pattern technique (see page 19). Remember to work the decs every 4th rnd.

Sew hem stitches down loosely to the inside without casting off.

Finishing: *Hems:* When you have about 40% of [K] sts left, and have achieved the depth you want, work 1 rnd MC, then purl 1 rnd to turn the hem. Switch to a lighter weight wool and knit about 2" (5 cm) in some startling color. You will need to inc at the 8 dec points to assure that the periphery of the hem will match the circumference of the body. With a nice sharp sewing-up needle, sew the raw sts down loosely on the inside without casting off. Work similar hems (without the shaping) on cuffs and lower edge by knitting up the sts from behind the cast-on (see page 21), thus eliminating the need for a purl rnd. Use a lighter weight wool if possible, or if you must use the sweater wool, dec 10% on the 2nd rnd of the hem as follows: *K8, k2tog; rep from *. *Tip:* Work the last rnd of the hem in the color to which it will be sewn. Sew the hem down neatly and loosely right off the needles as you did for the neck.

Weave the underarms. *Tip:* With fabric coming from three directions at the corners of the underarm, usually there is a hole. Before weaving, pick up a loose strand at each corner (top and bottom, left and right), twist it, and put it on the needle to be woven as a st. This adds 2 sts to be woven to each sleeve and to each side of the body. This should take care of the hole. If not, work duplicate st (see page 15) around the hole to close it up.

Aspen Yoke Sweater

MY FIRST GUEST APPEARANCE AS A DESIGNER IN Elizabeth's *Wool Gathering* was September 1972 when a sweater I had knitted several years before, the Aspen Yoke pullover, was featured. I used a single motif from Elizabeth's allover Shaded Aspen Leaf design, elongated the shape slightly, and shaded the background of the yoke behind the stems of the leaves. The Unspun Icelandic wool is a perfect material because it can be shaded so subtly.

Finished size

40 (42, 44)" (101.5 [106.5, 112] cm) bust/chest circumference.

Yarn

Unspun Icelandic wool (100% wool; 300 yd/3.5 oz): MC, 7 (7, 8) wheels, CC1, CC2, CC3, CC4, 1 wheel each.

Needles

Approximately size 7 (4.5 mm), plus one size smaller if you choose ribbing: 16" and 24" (40- and 60-cm) circular and set of double-pointed (for cuffs). Adjust needle size to obtain correct gauge.

Gauge

16 sts = 4" (10 cm); 4 sts = 1" (2.5 cm), with yarn doubled (pull 1 strand from the center and 1 strand from the outside of the wheel).

Note: [K] = 160 (168, 176) sts. See Elizabeth's Percentage System on page 16.

Body: With MC and 24" (60-cm) needle, cast on 152 (160, 168) sts. Join, being careful not to twist sts. Knit straight for 3" to 4" (7.5 to 10 cm). Mark 3 side "seam" sts diametrically opposed, and inc 1 st each side of each "seam"—4 sts inc'd. Work 3" to 4" (7.5 to 10 cm) straight and then rep this inc once more—160 (168, 176) sts (100% of [K]). Work straight to desired length to underarm, incorporating a set of short rows across the back if desired (see page 22). Place about 8% of [K]—13 (13, 15) sts— on waste wool at each underarm, centered above the side incs.

Edge variation: If you'd rather have plain or corrugated ribbing or garter st at the lower edge, cast on 144 (152, 158) sts. Work k1, p1 ribbing for a few inches, then increase to 100% [K] in the first stocking-st rnd. *Or* work back and forth in garter stitch—you will have to sew a short seam when

you're done—and at desired length join into a rnd, being careful not to twist sts, and increase to 100% [K] in the first stocking-st rnd.

Sleeves: With CC1 and double-pointed needles, cast on 20% of [K]—32 (36, 36) sts. Join, being careful not to twist sts. For a hem (shown on man's sweater, page 33), follow cuff chart. Mark center 3 underarm "seam" sts and inc 1 st each side of "seam" every 5th rnd until you have about 37% of [K]—60 (62, 64) sts. Work straight to desired sleeve length.

If you worked ribbing/garter on the body and want to match the cuffs, cast on 20% of [K]—32 (34, 36) sts—and work k1, p1 plain or corrugated ribbing, or garter st for desired cuff length. Change to stocking st and inc as follows.

Small: [k4, M1] around—8 incs, 40 sts.
Medium: k4 [M1, k7] 4 times, M1, k4, M1—6 incs, 42 sts.
Large: [k4, M1] 4 times, [k5, M1] 4 times—8 incs, 44 sts.

Tip: Work the final rnd of corrugated rib without any purl sts. When you inc in the next rnd, you can inc by knitting into the back of the st of the row below (see page 19), and you won't have to deal with purl bumps. Work about 4" to 5" (10 to 12.5 cm) plain. Work incs each side of marked underarm sts as above until you have about 37% of [K]—60 (62, 64) sts. Now knit straight to desired sleeve length. Place about 8% of [K]—13 (13, 15) sts on holders at underarms of each sleeve, centered over the shaping.

Knit the sleeves onto the body, matching underarms. You will have [K] + upper sleeve × 2, minus 4 × 8%—228 (240, 252) sts, a perfect multiple of 19 (20, 21) 12-st leaves.

Work one or two rnds plain. Shape the back of the neck as follows: knit around left sleeve and continue to 12 sts past sleeve/body join. Wrap (see "Short rows and wrapping" page 22), turn, and work back to the same point past the right sleeve/body join. Wrap the next st and turn. *Work to 10 sts shy of last wrap and wrap again. Rep from * 3 more times (a total of 3 sets of short rows). Knit around on all sts, working the wraps tog with their slipped sts.

Join CC1 and, centering the point of a leaf on the front, follow the chart, beg as indicated for your

Yoke

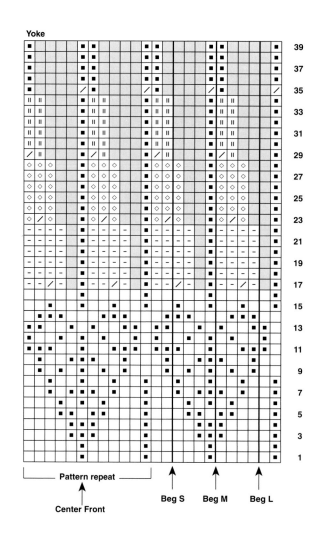

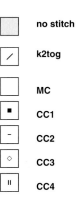

no stitch

k2tog

MC

CC1

CC2

CC3

CC4

Cuff

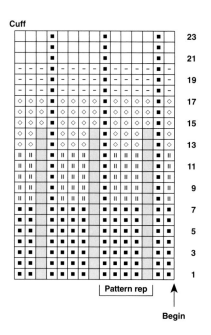

size. When the leaf is finished, the stems will continue to the neck and you will work decreases between them, shading the background as indicated and switching to a 16" circular needle when necessary. Work a final decrease rnd to obtain about 40% of [K] for the neck opening—64 (68, 70) sts.

Finishing: *Neck edging:* With smaller size needles, work k1, p1 ribbing for a turtleneck and bind off loosely, or purl 1 rnd (turning ridge) and work a hem to desired length with a single strand of Icelandic. If you make the hem very deep, you will need to increase the hem sts to match the diameter of the yoke where the hem will be sewn down. Sew raw sts to inside of neckline. Weave the underarm sts tog with the Kitchener stitch (see page 19).

If you chose hems for the borders, use smaller size needles and knit up sts around the lower edge of body and cuffs with a single strand of Icelandic and work hems to desired length, with or without a pattern or a message to the wearer. Sew down the raw sts lightly as described on page 22.

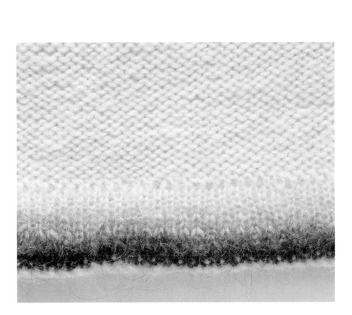

The inside of your hem may be shaded as shown here or carry a message.

ELIZABETH DESIGNED THE ALLOVER Shaded Aspen Leaf sweater for my first ski trip to Aspen when I was in high school. In the hem she knitted "Eleanor Fewmet," one of our family jokes. When we were small, Elizabeth had read aloud to us *The Once and Future King* by T. H. White. In the first book of the quartet, King Pellinore and his wretched bratchet's search for the Questing Beast instigated hysterical laughter from us all, especially because of the bag of fewmets the king used to keep the dog on the scent. Okay. Years later. In the late 1950s, long-distance telephone calls were considered an excessive extravagance. When traveling, to let our parents know we had arrived safely, we would call home, person-to-person to Eleanor Fewmet. Elizabeth might say, "I'm sorry but Miss Fewmet has just stepped into the tub," or some other unlikely activity. (Maybe you hadda be there.)

Russian Prime

THE MYSTERIOUS EFFECT THAT A BIAS COLOR pattern has on the ratio of stitches to rows was first demonstrated to me over a decade ago when I began knitting sweaters, coats, and stockings using diagonal Turkish color charts. As opposed to the five-to-seven ratio with which I was familiar, suddenly the ratio of stitches and rows to one inch was practically the same. At first I thought it was due to my relaxed gauge, but, in her Fair Isle book, Alice Starmore anticipates an identical stitch and row gauge in *any* stranded fabric, and her garments are firmly knitted.

This is one of those areas (along with my jogless circular color pattern [page 19], and 4-sided 3-stitch I-cord [page 18]) where I am sure there is a logical, analytical, and scholarly explanation to the mystery, but please don't tell me—I prefer to be amazed anew each time I use any of the above. Analysis can be destructive of magic things.

All right then. With this nearly-square ratio in mind, I plotted a drop-shoulder garment with sleeves knitted down from cut armholes, and the entire upper reaches of the body—from cuff to cuff—being (visually) an unbroken flow of pattern. Is knitting *great*, or what?

My pleasure at producing super-neat shaping-within-pattern at the undersides of sleeves has caused me to ruminate about putting the shaping down the *top* of the sleeve to show off the beautiful mirror-imaging. After all, you can raise your arm to scratch your head just so many times. In this instance it becomes an issue of Form Follows Function (my fave), because if I shape the sleeve down the center top, will that not cause the sleeve to angle down slightly, in a more anatomical manner? Yes, it will. *And*, what if I interrupt the main body pattern to produce side panels—may I not create a Kangaroo Pouch (see page 19) underarm and continue the side panels, unbroken, from lower body edge to cuff? Even so. *And* the side panels serve a dual purpose in that they allow me total freedom to produce the exact circumference I want without having a stitch count that is divisible by the pattern repeat, which can be very limiting. As long as the chart is centered front and back, I may begin knitting at any point within the repeat, and the

mirror-imaging before and after each side panel will form a design of its own and make a pleasing symmetry all around.

Quivering with excitement, I cast on. The unique pair of color-pattern charts featured here originate in Russia and came here via a Swedish book, kindly sent to me by Kay Crowthers, *Fiskartröjör Och Andra Tröjklassiker.* The charts embody a soothing repeat of numbers one, three, and five in a design the likes of which I had never before seen . . . Russian Prime, indeed. (Postscript: I was deflated to be told by a mathematician that "one" is not a prime number. I claim artistic license.)

RUSSIAN PRIME PULLOVER

This circular garment is constructed along the lines of a classic Norwegian dropped-shoulder sweater, with a few added details. Knitting begins at the lower edge of the body with either plain ribbing, corrugated ribbing, or a hem. If you choose ribbing, cast on fewer stitches, and increase to desired body circumference above the ribbing; establish the design and knit the body straight to desired length to underarm. If you decide on a hem, use the long-tail method (see page 14) to cast on fewer stitches, and take pleasure in increasing within the pattern as you work your way to desired circumference and length to underarm. The narrow side panels permit you to regulate the body circumference in small increments of 4 stitches despite the main 60-stitch pattern repeat.

At desired length to underarm, put the side panel stitches on a thread and cast on 5 steek stitches in their place, which you will keep in alternate colors. Work 2 plain rounds, 1 of MC and 1 of CC, then begin Yoke Chart, which maintains the 1, 3, 5 aspect, but is quite different in appearance. After an inch or so of the new chart, put the center-front 3 sts on a thread, cast on 5 steek stitches in their place (keeping them in alternate colors), and continue to about 3 to 4" (7.5 to 10 cm) shy of desired shoulder height. Place the front neck stitches on a holder and work a second steek, gently curving the neck opening by decreasing each side of the steek.

Continue straight to desired shoulder height. Put all stitches on a holder. Stitch and cut open all steeks, join shoulders, and knit up all stitches around armhole in pattern; pick up side panel stitches. Work sleeve down to the cuff, double-decreasing at the center top every 4 to 6 rounds (depending upon desired sleeve shape).

Work double I-cord (see page 18) around neck. I also worked single I-cord down the sleeve and into the cuff of the red version. Hem lower edge of body (if that is your choice), knitting in a secret message for the wearer. Done.

SPECIFIC INSTRUCTIONS

Note: The side panels require 13 sts each; the main body pattern is a 60-st repeat. The first round is a set-up round, and is not repeated. Find your size, establish 13-st side panel (SP), and begin set-up round, reading chart from right to left. The last st on the line is the pivot st: Knit it once, then knit the **same line** back from left to right. Repeat for back of garment.

Finished size

40 (42, 44, 46, 48)" (101.5 [106.5, 112, 117, 122] cm) bust/chest circumference. Length is up to you.

Yarn

Québécoise (100% wool; 210 yd/100 g): 5 (5, 6, 6, 6) skeins MC; 4 (4, 5, 5, 5) skeins CC.

Needles

Approximately size 6 (4 mm): 16" (40-cm) and 24 (60-cm) circular and set of double-pointed. Adjust needle size to obtain the correct gauge.

Gauge

22 sts = 4" (10 cm); 5½ sts = 1" (2.5 cm).

Ribbed version: With MC and 24" (60-cm) needle, CO 198 (210, 220, 228, 238) sts. Work k1b, p1 plain—or corrugated (which I wish I had done)—

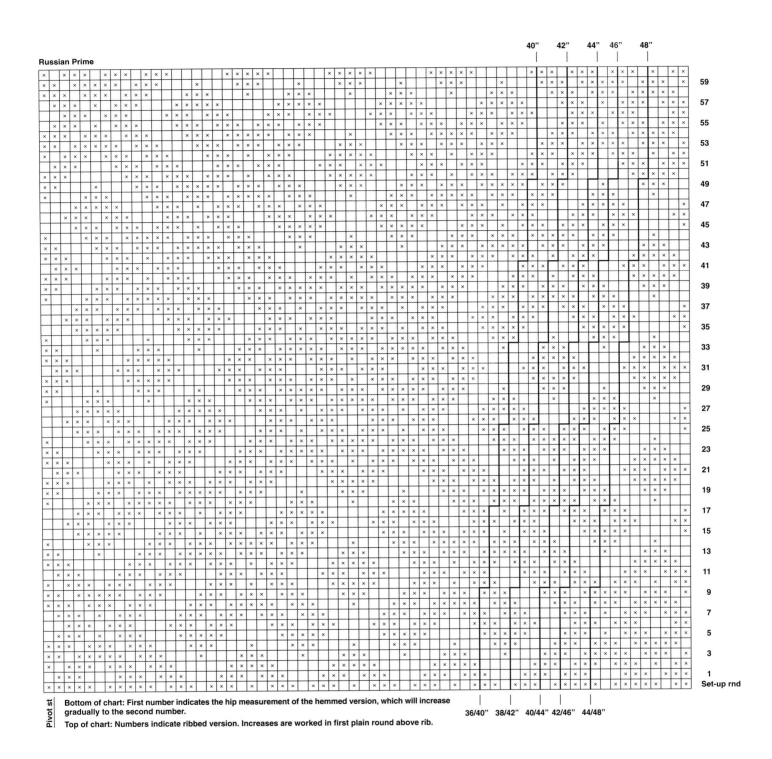

40" 42" 44" 46" 48"

59
57
55
53
51
49
47
45
43
41
39
37
35
33
31
29
27
25
23
21
19
17
15
13
11
9
7
5
3
1
Set-up rnd

Pivot st

Bottom of chart: First number indicates the hip measurement of the hemmed version, which will increase gradually to the second number.

Top of chart: Numbers indicate ribbed version. Increases are worked in first plain round above rib.

36/40" 38/42" 40/44" 42/46" 44/48"

☐ main color

☒ contrast color

ribbing, for 2 to 3" (5 to 7.5 cm). Increase in 1st plain round to [K] (see EPS page 16)—220 (232, 244, 252, 264) sts. To calculate an evenly-spaced increase, I recommend Cheryl Brunette's "More-or-Less Right Formula" in her book, *Sweater 101*. Locate your size at the top of the chart and run a highlight pen straight down to find your starting stitch on the set-up rnd. Establish main pattern front and back, plus the 2 side panels, and work straight to Rnd 60. Repeat from Rnd 1 and continue to desired body length. (Good stopping rnds are 21, 31, 41, and 51.)

Hemmed version: With 24" (60-cm) needle and using the long-tail method, CO 196 (208, 220, 228, 240) sts. Cause the outline stitch side of the cast-on to be the "right" side (see page 21) and establish main body pattern plus the 2 side panels. Follow the increases on the chart, and you will eventually arrive at [K]—220 (232, 244, 252, 264) sts at chest. Highlight on the chart the vertical path your chosen size requires. When you reach Rnd 60, repeat from Rnd 1 (making sure to follow your new path) to desired height to underarm. (Good stopping rnds are 21, 31, 41, and 51.)

I "signed" the red version in the left side panel.

Both versions underarm steek: Place the 13 side panel sts on a thread at each underarm. CO 5 sts in their place as a field for future cutting. Keep the 5 "steek" sts in alternate (speckled) colors. Knit 1 rnd MC, then 1 rnd CC. ***Begin yoke chart:*** After 5 to 8 rnds of the chart, place the center front 3 sts on a holder and CO 5 steek sts in their place. Keep the steek sts in alternate colors. When armhole measures 7½" (19 cm), ***make neck steek:*** Place 33 center front sts on a thread (14 + 5 steek sts + 14), CO 5 steek sts in their place, keeping them in alternate colors. ***Shape neck:*** Following dec lines on chart, *knit to within 2 sts of steek, k2tog, knit steek sts, ssk; rep from * 8 times total—16 sts eliminated. Cont straight until armhole measures 9 (9, 9½, 10, 10½)" (23 [23, 24, 25.5, 26.5] cm). Work final rnd in MC, casting off all steek sts as you go. Place all other sts on a thread. Baste down center of all 4 steeks. With small stitch and loose tension, machine stitch (very close to basting) down one side and up the other side of the steek. Cut on basting line. ***Join shoulders:*** Line up the front and back sts onto separate dpns. If you want an I-cord detail running down the length of the sleeve top, CO 3 sts (onto a 3rd needle). If you do not want I-cord on the sleeve, CO 2 sts. Beg at neck, work 3-needle I-cord cast-off as follows: *K2, sl 1, yo, k2tog (1 st each from front and back needles), p2so (the slipped st and the yo), place 3 sts back onto left needle. Repeat from * for all shoulder sts. Place the 3 cord sts on a thread.

I-cord continues down center top of sleeve to cuff.

Russian Prime Yoke

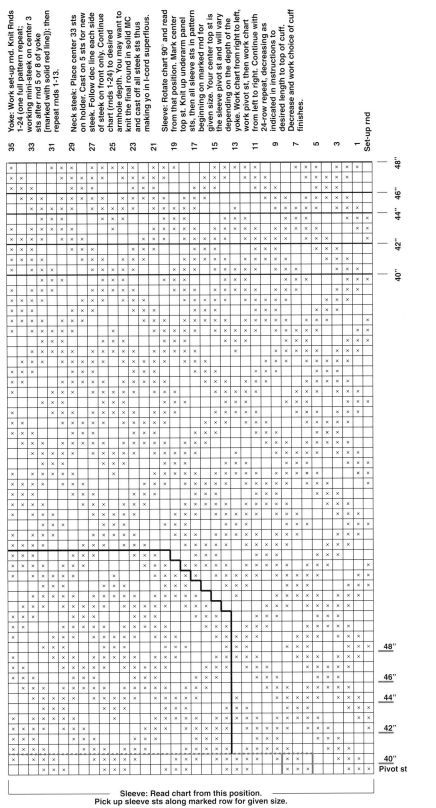

35   Yoke: Work set-up rnd. Knit Rnds 1-24 (one full pattern repeat; working mini-steek on center 3 sts after rnd 5 or 8 of yoke [marked with solid red line]); then repeat rnds 1-13.

29   Neck steek: Place center 33 sts on holder. Cast on 5 sts for new steek. Follow dec line each side of steek on front only. Continue chart (rnds 1-24) to desired armhole depth. You may want to knit the final round in solid MC and cast off all steek sts thus making yo in I-cord superfluous.

21   Sleeve: Rotate chart 90° and read from that position. Mark center top st. Knit up underarm panel sts, then all sleeve sts in pattern beginning on marked rnd for given size. Your center top st is the sleeve pivot st and will vary depending on the depth of the yoke. Work chart from right to left, work pivot st, then work chart from left to right. Continue with 24-row repeat, decreasing as indicated in instructions to desired length to top of cuff. Decrease and work choice of cuff finishes.

35 33 31 29 27 25 23 21 19 17 15 13 11 9 7 5 3 1 Set-up rnd

48" 46" 44" 42" 40"

48" 46" 44" 42" 40" Pivot st

Sleeve: Read chart from this position.
Pick up sleeve sts along marked row for given size.

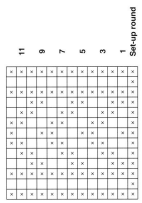

main color

× contrast color

---- mini steek: work to this line, work steek sts, then work back from this line

| center neck sts on hold; begin on rnd 5 or 8

Side panel

11 9 7 5 3 1 Set-up round

Sleeve: You may now continue the yoke pattern unbroken down the sleeve: Pick up the 13 side panel sts, and proceed to knit up 1 st for each row in pattern. I found the best results from knitting up *between* the last 2 vertical sts before the steek, pulling the required color up from below the fabric just to the left of your solid "size line," and duplicate the colors of the sts in the line that precedes it. Depending upon the size you are making, you will have approx 100–130 sleeve sts total.

At sleeve top: If sleeve cord is planned (shoulder I-cord continued down center top of sleeve to cuff), ignore the 3 sts on a thread for the time being, snag a thread from beneath the cord and mark it as the pivot stitch. If no sleeve cord is wanted, knit the 2 I-cord sts tog as you knit up sleeve sts, and mark that st to be the center top pivot stitch.

The side panel pattern continues uninterrupted along the sleeve underarm.

Turn your brain (chart) on its ear, identify your "starting line" on the Yoke/Sleeve chart, and off you go, working a double-decrease (sl 2tog kwise, k1, p2sso) at center top every 4th rnd for a tapered-to-the-cuff sleeve, every 5th rnd for a slightly full sleeve, or every 6th rnd for a bloused sleeve. Keep the dbl dec always in MC. (For bloused style, make sleeves 1 to 2" [2.5 to 5 cm] longer than desired so they will blouse.) At 2" (5 cm) shy of desired length, work a relatively severe decrease on the last rnd, depending upon the degree of "blouse" you have produced. You may find yourself working "k3,

k2tog around," "k2, k2tog," or even "k1, k2tog," heading (in the EPS mode [see page 16]) for approx 20–25% of [K] for cuff. Fudge a bit to keep the plain stripes each side of the underarm panel uninterrupted and allow them to flow into the cuff. Work ribbing for 2 to 3" (5 to 7.5 cm) on dpn. ***For continuous sleeve I-cord:*** After the sleeve is finished, pick up the 3 shoulder cord sts from their thread and work applied I-cord (see page 18) down the center-top sleeve stitch.

Finishing: *Neck trim:* With smaller needle and beg

I chose corrugated ribbing for the cuff on the blue version, working about 1" in all knit sts and 1" in k1, p1.

at lower neck opening, pick up 4 sts for every 5 rows up side of neck, all horizontal sts on thread, 4 for 5 for upper neck, all neck-back sts on thread, and mirror the foregoing on the other side. (I pick up about 20 sts, finish with I-cord, then pick up the next 20.) *I-cord:* Grab the 3 sts-on-a-thread at center front, and *k2, sl 1, yo, k1 (picked-up st), p2so (the slipped st and the yo), replace to left needle. The addition of a yo to my original 3-needle I-cord cast-off was "unvented" by Joyce Williams and prevents the CC from peeking through the cord. Repeat from * up one side. At neck corner, work an unattached round of cord each side of corner st (to provide enough fabric to turn 90°). Attach all sts when traveling horizontally. Cont in this manner to shoulder seam. Work a gentle dec across the neck-back sts by working a k2tog on every 5th and 6th st (to prevent flaring). ***Second layer of cord:*** Pick up 1 stitch for every row along just-knitted cord. With

CC, CO 3 sts at center front. *K2, sl 1, yo, k1, p2so (the slipped st and the yo), replace to left needle; rep from * up edge. At corner, work unattached rows as above, and swing the 2nd layer of cord to the *body* side of the 1st cord. Cont around neck to second corner. Climb up over 1st cord to finish 2nd layer on outside edge. Tack tog 1 to 2" (2.5 to 5 cm) of the neck opening. **Hem:** With MC and working into the purl bumps behind the outline st, knit up 1 st for every cast-on st and work 1 rnd. Dec 10% of the sts (k8, k2tog around). Knit the hem to desired depth (knitting in secret message if desired). Do not cast off. Slide about 20 sts off the needle at a time, and sew down to inside of body with sharp sewing-up needle: Skim through back of body fabric, then go through raw sts. Tack down the cut edges of the armholes and the neck front. Darn in all ends.

What a journey, eh?

Picky-Picky Department: When shaping the sleeves of the Russian Prime, you may want to rearrange matters in the round preceding the double-decrease to cause the 3 center sts to *all* be in MC; this prevents any CC from peeking through.

At the neck corner, work unattached second cord and swing it to the body side of the first cord.

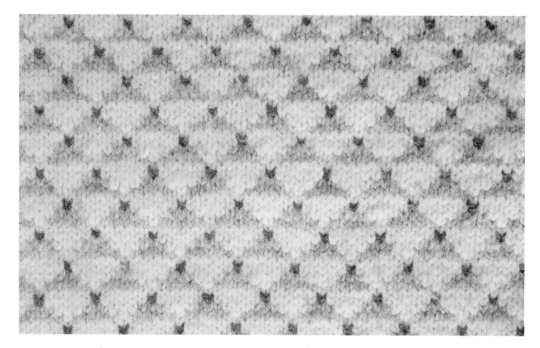

Faroese Sweater Variations

DECADES AGO, WHILE SAILING FROM HAMBURG to Reykjavik, my friend Hanna and I spent a day in the Faroe Islands when the ship stopped to unload cargo. Being a raw, knitting-illiterate youth, I did not scrabble about to research and absorb the rich, unique knitting history of the area; we went to a local dance instead. In memory, I liken the Faroese coastal landscape to sections of Oregon where in 1990, Camera Guy and I went to knit and videotape a Faroese sweater. By the way, the name of that remote group of islands, all alone in the North Sea between the Shetlands and Iceland, translates to "sheep islands." Nice, huh? Although the islands belong to Denmark, the Faroese have a language unto themselves, understood by neither Danes nor Icelanders but, we are told, distantly related to Old Norse. By the way again, our person-in-the-islands spells it Faroe, not Faeroe as some maps and books say.

Traditional Faroese garments are distinguished by their small, simple allover color patterns. Samples of these sweaters were exhibited in Copenhagen in 1927, and Queen Alexandrina was so entranced that she requested the pattern charts be incorporated into a book. That was done by Hans Debes, and the historic book *Foroysk Bindingarmynstur* remains in print to this day. As you knit the small patterns, they quickly transmit their "song" to you; if you, like me, choose to knit three different designs into your garment, the changing rhythms will keep you captivated and your sweater will be finished before you know it.

Like its cousin the Norwegian Luskofte, a traditional Faroese sweater is recognizable at a distance: nearly always a dropped-shoulder turtleneck pullover, nearly always knitted in natural undyed sheep's wool, and nearly always covered by a small-repeat color pattern.

I approached this design by knitting a long swatch of all my favorite Faroese color patterns. After scrutinizing the swatch for several days, I finally selected my three favorites and decided to use them all by putting one on the front, another on the back, and the third on the sleeves. This makes

the finished garment non-traditional, but adds great visual interest and provides entertaining variety for the knitter. For knitting in the round, the front and back patterns must be in color sync.

I have strayed from the authentic shape by putting hems at the lower edges instead of ribbing; by making a modified (slightly inset) armhole instead of a straight drop shoulder; by shaping a scooped neck instead of adding a turtleneck; and by knitting the sleeves into the body instead of sewing them. Also, since we were on the road during the knitting and taping of this design, I couldn't readily find a sewing machine, so I cut the armholes without any preliminary stitching—very exciting for this knitter! And I am pleased to report that after several years of wearing and washing, the cut (wool) edges remain secure and unraveled. For those vacationers of little faith, you can always machine stitch along the cut edges when you arrive back home.

Both the modified armhole shape and the lowered neck provide an opportunity for steeks: under-arm and neck-front stitches are put on a piece of wool, and extra stitches are cast on in their place as a cutting field, enabling you to continue knitting in the round from lower edge to shoulder height.

The instructions that follow will give you five sizes using the construction details outlined above. The prototype was made for my son Cully, and has a 40" (101.5 cm) hip circumference that increases at the side "seams" to a 44" (112-cm) chest. Decide if you want the body to expand or go straight as you head for the desired length to underarms.

Finished size

(Rounding off the half-measures in width): 36" hips increasing to 40" chest, (38/42, 41/45, 45/49, 47/51)" (92/102 [97/107, 104/115, 115/125, 120/130] cm). Length is up to you: approx. 26 (27, 28, 28, 28)" (66 [69, 71, 71, 71] cm). Armhole depth: 9½ (9½, 10, 10, 10½)" (24 [24, 26, 26, 27] cm).

Yarn

Unbleached 2-ply Sheepswool (210 yd/4 oz skein): 5 (5, 6, 6, 7) skeins cream (MC); 2 (2, 3, 3, 4) skeins pale gray (CC1), and 1 (1, 2, 2, 2) skeins black-sheep (CC2).

Needles

Approximately size 6 (4 mm): 16" (40-cm) and 24" or 29" (60-cm) circular and set of four double-pointed for cuffs. Adjust needle size to obtain the correct gauge.

Notions

Magnetic Row Finder (optional) to keep your place on the chart, although you will quickly memorize these patterns; 1 oz (28 g) lightweight wool for hems.

Gauge

18 sts and 28 rows = 4" (10 cm); 4½ sts and 7 rows = 1" (2.5 cm). If your row gauge doesn't match, no matter; just go by actual measurement.

Notes: To center the front pattern, you need an uneven number with a single center stitch. The back design requires an even number with two center stitches. Keep this in mind if you are working with your own numbers for sizes other than the ones given.

Don't worry if the pattern repeat does not fit evenly into your number of stitches; as long as the motifs are perfectly centered fore and aft, the partial pattern each side of the seam stitches will make a pleasing design of its own. And, if you are shaping the body from hem to armhole, partial side patterns are inevitable.

Ready? With 24" (60-cm) needle and using the long-tail (see page 14) method (to facilitate the hem later), CO 161 (169, 185, 201, 209) sts (the lower edge will be 4" [10 cm] narrower than the chest circumference). Mark 5 sts at each side "seam" for the vertical dividers between front and back, and work them in alternate colors throughout: L(ight), D(ark), L, D, L. The rounds will start with these 5 seam sts.

To begin, the front pattern will have 75 (79, 87, 95, 99) sts, with 1 center st. The back pattern will have 76 (80, 88, 96, 100) sts, with 2 center sts. (If you'd rather have ribbing, CO the above number plus 1 and inc to desired chest measurement in 1st round above rib, then work straight to underarm. This will produce a ribbing that is snug around the hips, then blouses to body circumference while the hem hangs nearly straight.)

Join and knit 1 plain round. Establish the front and back patterns and work to desired length to underarm—approximately 17 (17½, 18, 18, 18)" (43 [44, 46, 46, 46] cm). Along the way, if you want to, **Shape the body:** At about 4" (10 cm) from CO edge: knit in pattern to marked side sts, M1, k5 (L, D, L, D, L), M1. Repeat at other side. Following chart, work straight and repeat the increases at 3" (7.5-cm) intervals, incorporating the new sts into

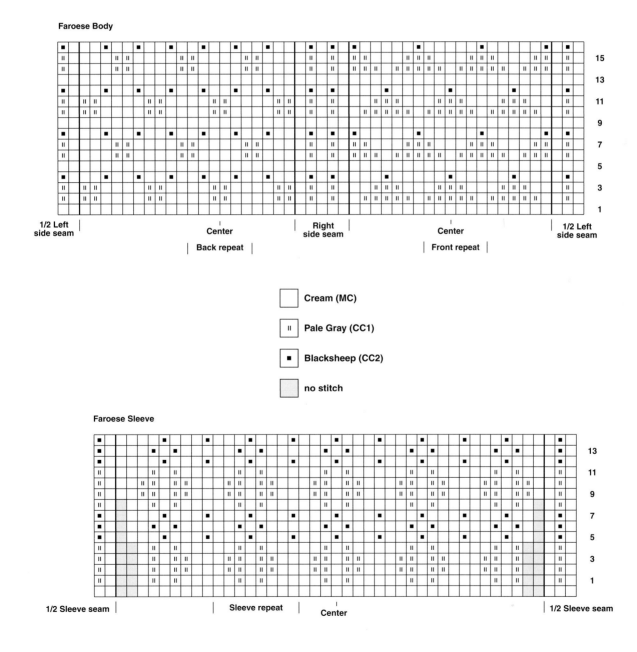

Faroese Body

1/2 Left side seam · Center · Right side seam · Center · 1/2 Left side seam

Back repeat · Front repeat

☐ Cream (MC)

‖ Pale Gray (CC1)

▪ Blacksheep (CC2)

▨ no stitch

Faroese Sleeve

1/2 Sleeve seam · Sleeve repeat · Center · 1/2 Sleeve seam

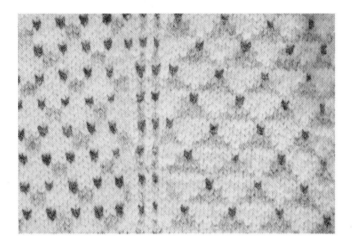

The body is increased along side "seams" and new stitches are incorporated into the front and back patterns.

the front and back patterns as warranted, until you have the desired number of chest sts, or [K] (see EPS page 16)—181 (189, 205, 221, 229) sts. Work straight until piece measures desired length to underarm—about 17 to 18" (43 to 46 cm). *Kangaroo pouch armholes:* Place 9 (9, 11, 11, 13) sts at each underarm, centered above the marked sts, on holder. Using the backward loop method (see page 12), CO 7 steek sts in their place and cont around, keeping steek sts in alternate colors as before.

You have total control over the degree to which the armhole will sink into the body. If you want less of a dropped shoulder, put a few more sts on the threads. I have 7 steek sts because I knew I would have to cut without machine-stitching first. If you have the security of a machine you may reduce the steeks to 5 sts each and save some wool.

Cont to 2" (5 cm) from desired height to shoulder. *Shape neck:* Place the center front 37 sts on a thread. CO 7 steek sts and cont around, keeping steek sts in alternate colors as before, for 2" (5 cm). (Note: Those 37 sts will make an 8" (20.5-cm) neck width for all sizes. I bordered the neck edge with a narrow I-cord, although you may substitute 1" (2.5 cm) of ribbing. Adjust the 37 sts according to desired neck width.) Work a final round of MC on all sts, casting off the armhole steek sts if you like. Put the front neck steek—and all other raw sts—on a holder.

Sleeves: *Cuff:* With dpn, CO 40 (40, 42, 42, 44) sts. Join and mark the center 5 underarm sts (to be

worked in L, D, L, D, L throughout. Establish (and center) the sleeve pattern. Inc 1 st each side of the underarm sts every 4 rnds, incorporating the inc'd sts into the design and switching to 16" (40-cm) cir needle when practical, until you have approximately 82 (86, 90, 90, 96) sts. Make sure the sleeve-top width fits the depth of the armhole. Work straight to within 1 (1, 1¼, 1¼, 1½)" (2.5 [2.5, 3.2, 3.2, 3.8] cm) shy of desired length to underarm. Work the final 1 to 1½" (2.5 to 3.8 cm) of sleeve back and forth in pattern, divided at center underarm. Do not cast off; leave the raw sts on the needle, or thread them onto a piece of wool.

Finishing: Baste down the center of each armhole steek. Machine stitch (if you have access to a sewing machine) each side of the basting with small stitch and loose tension. Cut the piece along basting. (Aside: with my unstitched garment, I became a bit paranoid and knitted up armhole sts before I cut the steek open.)

Join shoulders with 3-needle, 2-stitch I-cord cast-off as follows: Slide the front shoulder sts of one side onto a needle and pick up the same number of sts from the back body onto another needle. Hold the 2 needles parallel with insides facing. Onto a third needle, in MC, cast on 2 I-cord sts, and transfer them to one of the parallel needles. Working firmly, *k1 (cord st), sl 1 (2nd cord st), k2tog (1 st each from front and back needles), psso. Replace 2 cord sts on one of the parallel needles and rep from * across shoulder. Break wool and thread it through the 2 cord sts. Darn in end. Repeat for other shoulder. *For fussy knitters (FFK):* This beautiful ridged seam has a different appearance on each side. If you want the fronts to match, work the cast-off in the same direction. So if you knitted the first seam from armhole-to-neck, work the second from neck-to-armhole.

Join sleeves to body: From the first vertical line of body sts beyond the steek, pick up approximately 5 sts for every 6 rows around the armhole, plus all the raw underarm sts. You will invariably find sloppy threads at the corners. Pick up and twist these threads and treat them as sts; that applies to the neck opening as well. On the sleeve needle, pick up additional sts from the back-and-forth slit-sleeve selvedges to match the number of kangaroo pouch sts on body. Recount to make sure you have the same number of sleeve and armhole sts. Line up the sleeve needle with the armhole needle, and, beg at center underarm, work the 3-needle, 2-stitch I-cord cast-off across the brief underarm horizontal section and around the armhole (making sure the center top of the sleeve aligns with the shoulder seam); end with the second half of the horizontal slit section. Weave cord ends tog.

As you are attaching the sleeve, stay alert to your gauge—is the cord too firm or too loose? Make necessary adjustments by changing needle size so that the resulting join is just right. You want the shoulder seam firm to prevent stretching, but the armhole needs flexibility.

Join shoulders with the 3-needle, 2-stitch I-cord cast-off. (This version shows optional shoulder shaping.)

Neck edging: Remove the holding thread from the neck steek sts. Ravel all rows. Cut through the center of the resulting ladders. These ends will be darned in later and will provide smooth, flat neck sides. Now, with the 16" (40-cm) cir needle pick up all raw sts and knit up sts from the side sections. On a dpn, CO 2 cord sts and, beg at a shoulder corner, work 2-st I-cord cast-off as before. Dec slightly by knitting 2 picked-up sts tog every 6th or 7th st on neck back and sides. Weave ends of cord tog. (Note: To help prevent the neck edge from rolling, I varied the I-cord cast-off slightly, and I quite like the result: *P1, k2tog tbl, replace 2 sts to left needle; rep from * around.)

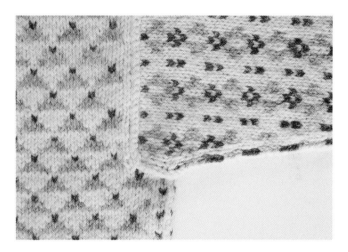

Stay alert to gauge when attaching sleeves to the body—the armhole needs flexibility.

Hems: With a lighter-weight wool (Shetland jumper-weight works beautifully), from behind the outline st of the long-tail CO, knit up 1 st for every cast-on st around the lower edge. Work 10 to 15 rnds in stocking st, knitting in a message if you choose. At desired hem depth, use a sharp needle to sew the raw sts down by skimming through the inside body fabric, then through the raw st. Maintain a straight horizontal line and keep it loose so the hem can breathe with the body sts. Repeat for cuffs . . . or not. My cuffs showed no sign of wanting to roll up, so I left them untreated. Darn in all ends. Block.

Turkish Maple and Turkish Ocean Pullovers

ARE THERE SUGAR MAPLE TREES IN TURKEY? I think not—and I would like to explain this possible anomaly. The main pattern in this sweater is Turkish. Initially I had a rough idea of the shape and layout of the design but, as I was pondering which colors to choose, my eye fell upon a favorite watercolor Chris had done of an autumn Sugar Maple in full regalia.

It is typical for people to stream to New England for fall foliage tours, but that area's spectacular autumn colors have nothing on ours; autumn's splendor is a well-kept secret here in central Wisconsin. The particular tree Chris painted was made up of masses of different reds with strong, dark brown branches and twigs. The palette was available in burgundy, barn red, scarlet, persimmon, coral, and natural black Shetland wool—so off I went.

With Schoolhouse's array of 160 shades of Shetland wool, you will have no difficulty substitut-

ing colors to suit your taste. Color combinations are endless. You might even consider using only two colors throughout while concentrating on the patterns.

This sweater is knitted in the round from the lower edge. Armholes are inset to the depth of the side panel pattern with extra steek sts cast on for an armhole cutting field; the rounded neck utilizes another steek. Sleeve sts are knitted up around the cut armhole, side panel raw sts are picked up, and the sleeve is worked to the cuff with shaping along each side of a wide underarm panel pattern, so the panels themselves continue uninterrupted from the lower body edge to the cuff, providing a field in which you can knit a name and date.

Lower borders of both body and cuffs use my Purl When You Can (PWYC) mode (see page 22). I wanted to knit a garment whose color pattern began immediately after casting on: no ribbing, no garter-stitch, no hem. So, as you work the border

pattern, whenever the chart calls for a stitch of one color above a like-colored stitch, purl it. (If you purl a stitch of one color into a contrasting color you will get the "dreaded purl blip"—which of course is a design feature in Swedish Bohus knitting). Originally I'd purl whenever the colors permitted, but further experiments have shown that fewer purl stitches are required than you may think. I now pick either the foreground or the background and PWYC in that color only to prevent lower-edge curl. As with corrugated rib, use either the cable (or knitted-on) method of casting on, or the German twisted method (see page 13).

Note: The Maple shading requires frequent color changes throughout the garment. I strongly recommend you get into the habit of splicing in each new color (see page 23). It takes a little time, but eliminates darning in a kazillion ends and keeps the inside of the garment as beautiful as the outside. The colors are so closely related that splicing one color with another is not noticeable and when you are done you have only the cast-on and the cast-off ends to darn in. Also, the Maple has ever-changing bands of shaded colors but the Ocean is one large shade—as always, knitter's choice.

Another note: The main diagonal pattern lends itself to shaping whereas the straight side panels do not. Since my son Cully is quite tapered, I worked the charts straight for a few inches, then increased as I knitted my way up the body: 1 stitch each side of the center pattern of both front and back (for a total of 4 new stitches) every few inches. I worked 4 sets of increases total (16 stitches). The new stitches are absorbed invisibly into the motif. *Or* increase suddenly in the plain round above the lower border pattern and work the body straight to underarms.

Finished size

S (M, L), rounding up the half-measures. 38" (97 cm) lower edge, increasing to 42" (107 cm) (40" inc to 45" [102 to 115 cm], 43" inc to 47" [109 to 120 cm]) body; 28" (71 cm) long, or desired length; sleeves about 22" (56 cm) or desired length. Alter your gauge to achieve the circumference you want; length is easily adjusted by measuring as you knit.

Yarn

Shetland Jumper-weight wool: Natural black #5 (MC), 8 (8, 9) oz. Plus 2 oz each barn red #1403, scarlet #93, persimmon #125, burgundy #55, and coral #129. Add another ounce of each color for a larger garment.

Needles

Approximately size 3 (4, 5) (3.25 [3.5, 3.75] mm): 24" (60-cm) and 16" (40-cm) circular and set of double-pointed. And needles 1 to 2 sizes smaller for lower border and cuffs. Adjust needle size to obtain the correct gauge.

Gauge

7 (6½, 6¼) sts -1" (2.5 cm)

Note: The colors are repeated in relatively narrow bands, about 5 to 7 rounds high: *barn red, scarlet, persimmon, coral, persimmon, scarlet, barn red, burgundy; rep from *. (You may need only 1 oz of the lightest and darkest reds.)

With MC and smaller needle, CO 266 sts. The border pattern is a 14-st repeat, so you will have 19 repeats (which you may bump down to 18 for a 252-st lower edge). Follow Border chart, working Purl When You Can; beginning with the lightest

This is an example of a PWYC border.

Turkish Maple

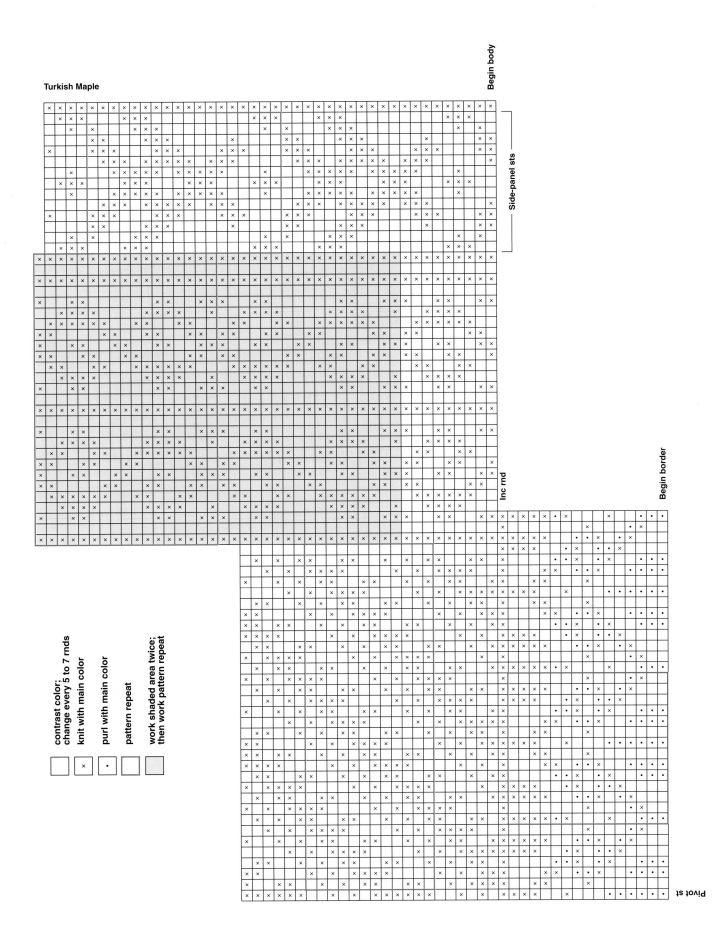

Begin body

Side-panel sts

Inc rnd

Begin border

Pivot st

contrast color;
change every 5 to 7 rnds

knit with main color

purl with main color

pattern repeat

work shaded area twice;
then work pattern repeat

Turkish Maple and Turkish Ocean Pullovers   53

background color, change colors every 3 rnds to get them all represented in the border. Now work 1 plain rnd MC, inc from 266 to 290 sts as follows: [k11, M1] 22 times, [k12, M1] 2 times; inc from 252 to 290 sts as follows: [k6, M1] 14 times, [k7, M1] 24 times. Follow the body chart, changing colors every 5 to 7 rounds to desired length to underarms. *Shape underarms:* Keeping 1 MC knit-up st at each side, place the 27 side-panel sts on a thread and CO 7 steek sts (work them in alternate speckles). Repeat at other underarm and cont in patt until piece measures about 2½" (6.5 cm) from desired height to shoulder. *Shape neck:* Place center 47 (more or less) sts on a thread and CO 7 steek sts. Cont around, dec 1 st each side of the steek sts every rnd as follows: [k2tog, k7 steek sts, ssk] 7 times, or until you have nibbled your way to the outer edge of the center chevron pattern. Now work straight to desired length to shoulder. Knit 1 final rnd in black, during which you may cast off the 3 sets of steek sts if you like. Place all sts on a thread.

Stitch and Cut: (Or as a first-time Camper said, "Stitch-and-omigod-cut".) Baste down the center of each steek. Machine stitch (with small stitch close to the basting thread) down one side and up the other. Cut on basting. Sew, weave, or use I-cord (see page 15) to join the shoulders.

Sleeve: Knit up sts around the armhole: 1 st for each rnd, pick up the raw underarm sts. (I had 136 sts: 54 on each side, 1 at the top, and 27 raw sts). The underarm panel will continue unbroken down the sleeve. Establish the point of the Turkish design at the center top shoulder st and work a quasi-gusset by dec each side of the underarm panel every

other row 9 times. Then dec every 5 or 6 rnds for a bit, then work straight for a while. Dec some more below the elbow. I ended up with 86 sts and nearly forgot to "sign" this sweater—just managed to squeeze it in above the cuff. *Bloused cuff:* At about 2" (5 cm) from desired length, work a plain rnd and dec severely to reduce the 86 sts to 56 sts (conveniently divisible by 14). Work the border chart, Purling When You Can, and lining up the center of the cuff pattern to meet the midline of the sleeve pattern. Very satisfying.

Note: It is a good idea to get both sleeves going at once . Knit a few inches on one sleeve then catch up with the other.

After working a 3-stitch I-cord cast-off around the neck, knit up sts between the I-cord and the body, then cast them off immediately. This helps prevent the neck edge from curling.

Finishing: With natural black, knit up and pick up all sts around the neck. Work a 3-stitch I-cord cast-off. That will not be sufficient to prevent the stocking st from curling, so, with burgundy, knit up sts all around neck just below the I-cord (between the cord and the body). Cast them right off. There.

Turkish Ocean Pullover

Finished Size

S (M, L), rounding up the half-measures. 38" lower edge, increasing to 45" (40" inc to 48", 43" inc to 50") (97 inc to 114.5 [102 inc to 122, 109 inc to 127] cm); body length: 28" (71 cm), or desired length; sleeve length: about 22" (56 cm), or desired length. Alter your gauge to achieve the circumference you want; length is easily adjusted by measuring as you knit.

Yarn

Shetland Jumper Weight wool, 8 (8, 9) oz cream (MC), plus 2 oz each loch maree prussian blue, deep teal, teal, turquoise, pale turquoise. Add another ounce of each color for a very long/wide garment.

Needles

Approximately size 3 (4, 5) (3.25 [3.5, 3.75] mm): 24" (60-cm) and 16" (40-cm) circular and set of double-pointed. Needles 1 to 2 sizes smaller for lower border and cuffs. Adjust needle size to obtain the correct gauge.

Gauge

7 (6½, 6¼) sts to-1" (2.5 cm).

Shading: From darkest to palest, about 3 inches/18 rnds of each color, excluding blending rnds. To blend the colors, I worked 1 rnd of the new shade, 2 rnds of previous shade, 2 rnds of new, 1 rnd of previous, then all new shade.

With smaller needle and darkest color, CO 266 sts. The border pattern is a 14-st repeat, so you will have 19 repeats (which you may bump down to 18 for a 252-st lower edge, which I did). Follow Border chart, working Purl When You Can (see page 22) in darkest color only. Now knit 1 plain rnd with MC, inc to 316 sts as follows. From 252 sts: K1, M1, [k4, M1] 31 times, k2, [M1, k4] 31 times, M1, k1. From

266 sts: K6, [M1, k5] 25 times, k3, [k5, M1] 25 times, k7. Follow the body chart to desired length to underarms.

The side panel pattern continues along the sleeve underarm, with shaping on either side.

Place side panels (23 sts each) on a thread/holder and CO 5 steek sts. Cont in patt to within 2 to 2½" (5 to 6.5 cm) of desired height to shoulder.

Saddle notes: Preferring knitting over sewing, I like to knit the saddle directly onto the raw body sts. However, when you're working a 2-color saddle, there is usually an unsightly join where the perpendicular fabrics meet. Joyce Williams has solved this problem by incorporating Elizabeth's 2-stitch built-in I-cord (see page 18) along each saddle edge.

Since I am not adept at purling back in color-pattern, I choose to KBB (knit back backward, see page 19) and you may want to experiment with that. Those familiar with intarsia know that the carried color must be twisted or "trapped" at each edge of a motif before you work back in the other direction. You will eventually develop your own method of

The saddle begins at the center back and is worked out toward the shoulders.

Turkish Ocean

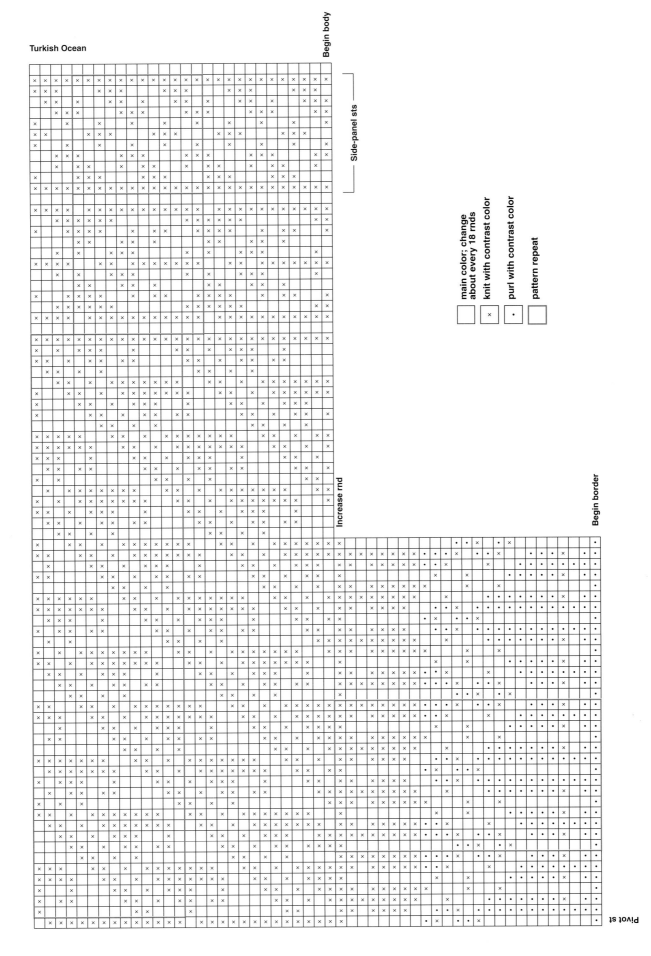

Begin body

Side-panel sts

main color; change about every 18 rnds

knit with contrast color

purl with contrast color

pattern repeat

Increase rnd

Begin border

Pivot st

Turkish Maple and Turkish Ocean Pullovers   57

execution, but essentially you want to place the carried color *over* the MC before heading back.

This diagonal fabric is nearly square. To keep the saddle lying nice and flat, nibble away 2 body sts tog with 1 saddle st at each edge. I recommend that you prepare for the saddle in advance by working a final plain round of k2tog across the saddle portion of the round, excluding the 47 neck front and the 10 armhole steek stitches. Put all sts on a thread/holder. Baste and machine st armholes (see page 20), but do not cut them open yet.

The saddle is worked on a total of 41 sts (37 saddle + 2 I-cord sts at each side) for a 4¼" wide saddle. To lower the neck back slightly, cast on approximately ⅓ of the total saddle sts, plus 2 for I-cord edging.

So. The body sts are on a piece of wool. (Actually, I leave the holder wool in place as I work the saddle and whip it out with a flourish when I am finished). The saddle begins at center back and is worked toward left shoulder. The right side of the first section of saddle is a selvedge and the left side will be knitted onto the back body sts, incorporating a 2-st I-cord. Find a pair of dpn and use the invisible method (see page 13) to CO 14 (12 + 2 cord sts) sts. Join in CC and keep first and last sts, plus I-cord sts in CC throughout saddle.

Right Side: *Following chart, work in patt to last 3 sts. Slide 1 body st from holder onto left needle and k2tog. Knit last 2 (I-cord) sts. Turn.

Purl Side: Wyif, sl 2 sts pwise. Trap the carried color on the first st and work (in patt) to end of row. Turn. Repeat from *.

When you have worked to the edge of the neck opening, cast on to the selvedge edge (invisibly or not) 27 sts—the rest of the saddle + 2 cord sts. You now have 37 + 4 total. Turn.

**Right side*: K2 (cord sts), sl 1 kwise, sl 1 front body st from holder kwise, knit 2 sl sts tog. Work saddle to within last 3 sts. Slide 1 body st from holder onto left needle and k2tog. Knit last 2 (I-cord) sts.

Purl side: Wyif, slip 2 sts pwise, work to within last 2 sts. Wyif, slip 2 pwise. Turn. Repeat from **.

Continue saddle to armhole edge and, with another needle, knit up 1 st for each rnd around armhole, including the underarm panel sts. The saddle pattern will now be continued on the circular sleeve and the I-cord edges will be abandoned. The sleeve and cuff shaping is the same as for the Turkish Maple.

The other half of the saddle and sleeve will be a mirror-image of the foregoing. Return to center back neck and pick up 14 invisibly cast-on sts and work right saddle as for left, reversing shaping. Work sleeve as for left.

Admittedly, the saddle is a bit of a challenge, but if you persevere, you will become familiar with the moves and find your own rhythm. Remember, you can always cop out, eliminate the saddle altogether, and finish the Ocean in the same manner as the Maple.

Finish the neck edge with 2- or 3-st I-cord.

Finishing: Apply 2 or 3-st I-cord to neck edge. Knitter's choice.

Turkish Ocean

Left back neck, saddle, and sleeve top

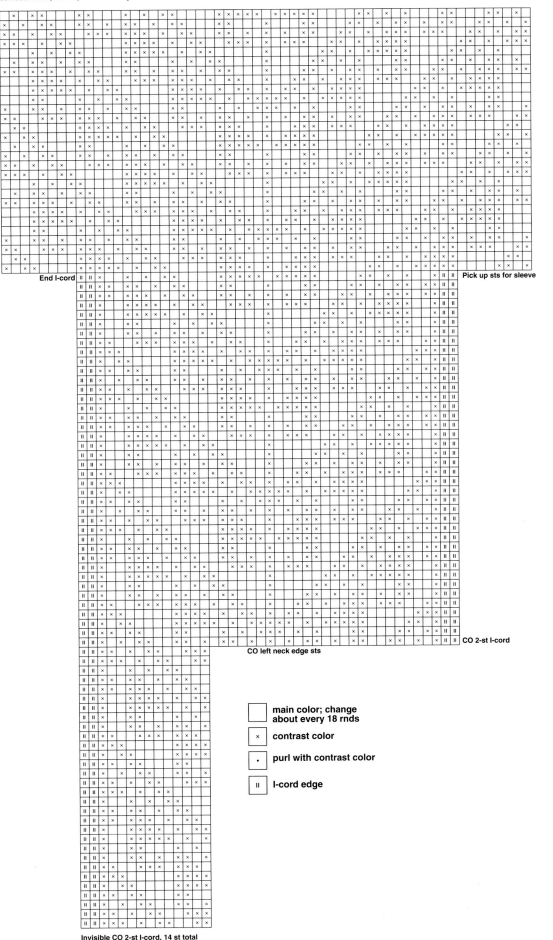

End I-cord

Pick up sts for sleeve

CO 2-st I-cord

CO left neck edge sts

□ main color; change about every 18 rnds

× contrast color

• purl with contrast color

‖ I-cord edge

Invisible CO 2-st I-cord, 14 st total

Celtic Swirl

THE SINUOUS AND INTRIGUING PATTERNS associated with all things Celtic continue to enchant designers using myriad mediums, most certainly including wool and needles. All the projects I have designed and knitted in this mode have been based on charts from a dear little book by Co Spinhoven, *Celtic Charted Designs* (Dover, 1987).

For this pullover, using the Stitch Painter program, I grabbed a narrow horizontal section where Co's vertical swirls meet each other, then "rubber-stamped" it in layers to get the pattern that forms the lower ribbing. That was all I had to start with; from then on it was seat-of-my-pants knitting.

Since the PWYC (see page 22) border section melted into the main body pattern, I couldn't increase above it without causing misalignment, so I began on a two-sizes-smaller circular needle. After three vertical repeats of the border pattern (with dark red as the main color and the background shifting from silver gray to ashes of roses to dusty rose to pink mix to raspberry and back again) I switched to the body-size needle and, following the swirl chart, motored up to desired length to underarm.

The original swirls are in pairs—facing up or down—but the 58-stitch repeat is rather unwieldy. Ideally you will require a number of stitches that equals an even number of pairs. I was not so lucky and worked in 29-stitch half-swirls. With a total of five sets of swirls around the body, my side "seams" fall in mid-swirl, and caused me to do a mental hiccough at each side.

Finished size

S (M, L), beginning on smaller needle, then switching to larger size, 33" hip/36" chest (41/45, 50/54)" (84/92 [104/115, 127/137] cm), rounding up the half-measures.

Yarn

Shetland Jumper-weight wool: dark red (MC), 7 (7, 8) oz; silver gray, ashes of roses, 2 (2, 3) oz each; dusty rose, pink mix, raspberry, 1 oz each.

Needles

Approximately size 4 (3.5 mm) 24" or 29" (60- or 80-cm) and 16" (40-cm) circular and set of double-pointed needles, and 1 to 2 sizes smaller for lower border and cuffs. Adjust needle sizes to obtain the correct gauge.

Gauge

Body: 26 sts = 4" (10 cm) in color pattern on larger needles. Lower border and cuffs: 28 sts = 4" (10 cm) on smaller needles.

Note: I knitted every other swirl in silver gray and shaded the alternate swirls as follows: of the 29 rounds, I knitted 5 rounds in ashes of roses, 4 in dusty rose, 4 in pink mix, 3 in raspberry, 4 in pink mix, 4 in dusty rose, and 5 in ashes of roses.

Body: With smaller size 24" or 29" (60-or 80-cm) circular needle, CO 232 (290, 348) sts. Beginning with PWYC (see page 22), follow border chart, beginning as indicated for your size. Change to larger size needle and work body chart to desired length to underarm.

From here on you are encouraged to make your own design decisions. I will tell you what I did for the size medium: At the underarm I put 28 sts (one swirl) on a thread at each underarm and cast on 7 steek sts (which I kept in speckles throughout). Then I put it aside for a week to cogitate.

If you are knitting the large size, you may want to put more sts on the underarm thread. Decide how far you want the sleeve to set into the body—but don't go too far or you will have to work the shoulder cap back and forth before joining the sleeve into a circle.

I repeated the lower border pattern for the yoke and played with colors in an almost random way (eliminating the raspberry). Since I had inset the armhole by 14 sts I made it deeper than usual—about 10½ to 11" (26.5 to 28 cm). At about 8½" (21.5 cm) above the armhole steek, I put the center 51 sts on a thread for the bottom of the neck opening and cast on 7 steek sts. *However*, before I did that, anticipating an I-cord neck border, the rnd before the steek I knitted the 51 center-front sts all in MC (dark red) trapping in the CC along the way. On the subsequent round I ran a piece of wool through the 51 raw sts and cast on 7 steek sts. For a bit of neckline shaping, dec 1 st each side of steek every rnd 5 times, then work straight to desired length to shoulder. With insides facing, join shoulders with the 3-needle cast-off (see page 15), worked with back facing from left shoulder to neck and then from neck to right shoulder.

What to do about the sleeves? Swirl patterned? Yoke patterned? Solid MC with patterned cuffs? I actually knitted seven (yes, 7) sleeves before settling on what you see here. And, to tell the truth, I'm not crazy about the result, but I was thoroughly sick of knitting sleeves.

Sleeves: Pick up the underarm sts (±28) and knit up sts around the armhole. I had 62 sts on each side and 1 at center sleeve top—153 sts total. Begin sleeve-band chart, but work a double-dec at center sleeve top on the very first rnd. Keep the underarm sts in 2/1 stripes. Establish a double-dec at each underarm corner and work it every rnd 7—125 sts. Now switch the decrease location to the top of the sleeve; establish diagonal stripes (5/1) after the pattern band is finished and double-dec every 5th rnd (or every time there are 3 stripe sts together at the top) 7 times—105 sts. Work straight to about 3" (7.5 cm) below elbow length (if you want a bloused

Celtic Border, Body, and Sleeve cuff

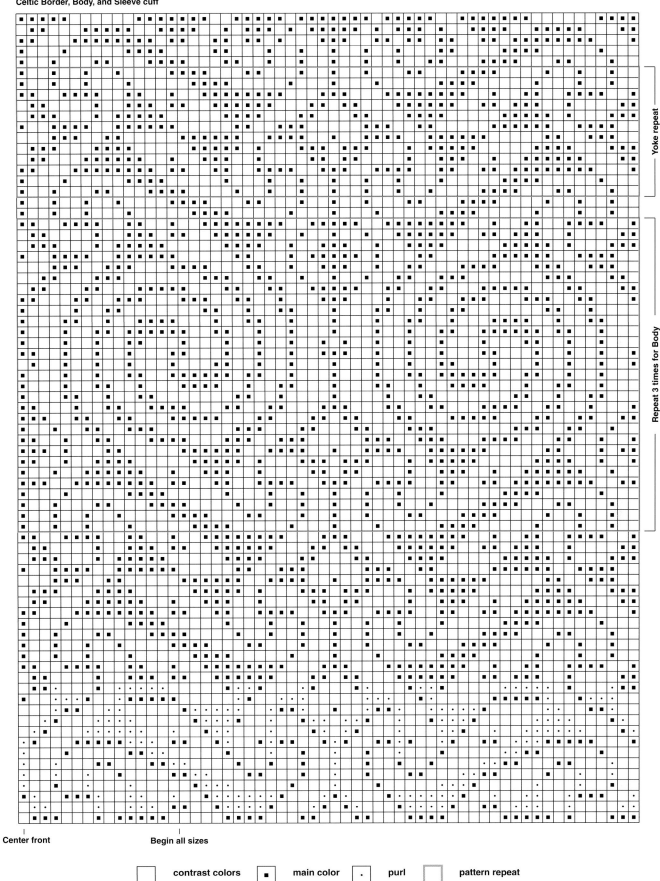

Yoke repeat

Repeat 3 times for Body

Center front

Begin all sizes

contrast colors ■ main color · purl pattern repeat

Keep the underarm stitches in 2/1 stripes.

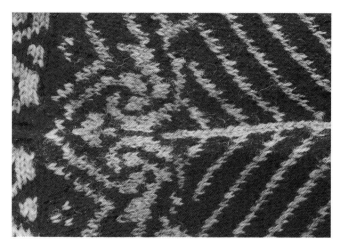

Once the top-of-sleeve band is finished, switch decrease location to the top of the sleeve and establish 5/1 diagonal stripes.

sleeve, be sure to knit it a few inches too long to allow it to pouffe) and work 1 rnd plain MC during which you dec severely to 58 sts and knit the deep cuff—this one is 7½" (19 cm) long. Purl 2 rnds in MC and cast off.

Neck: Pick up and knit all sts. Decrease 6 to 8 sts across back neck. I ended up with about 140 sts. Purl 1 rnd and work Elizabeth's sewn casting off (see page 15).

contrast colors

main color

purl

pattern repeat

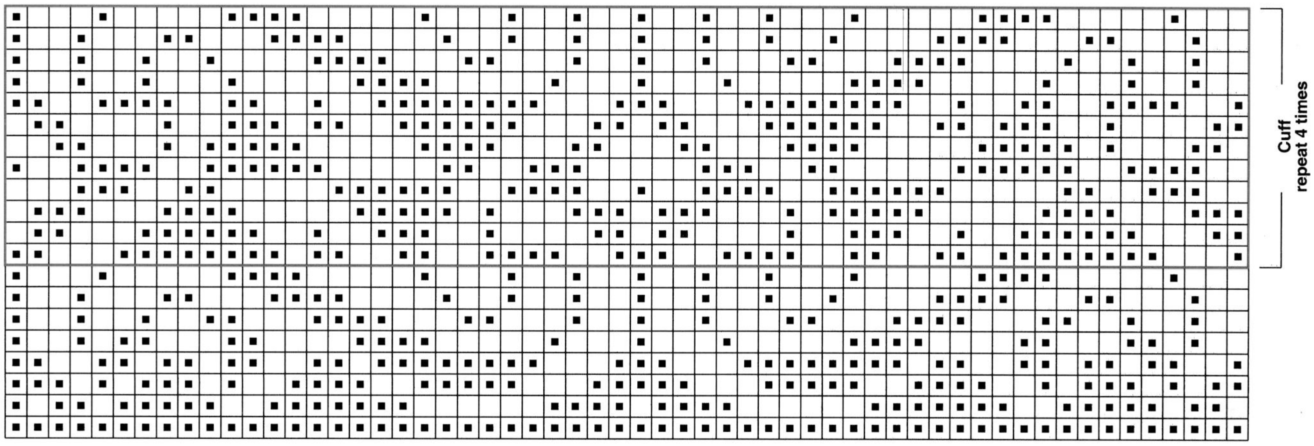

Cuff
repeat 4 times

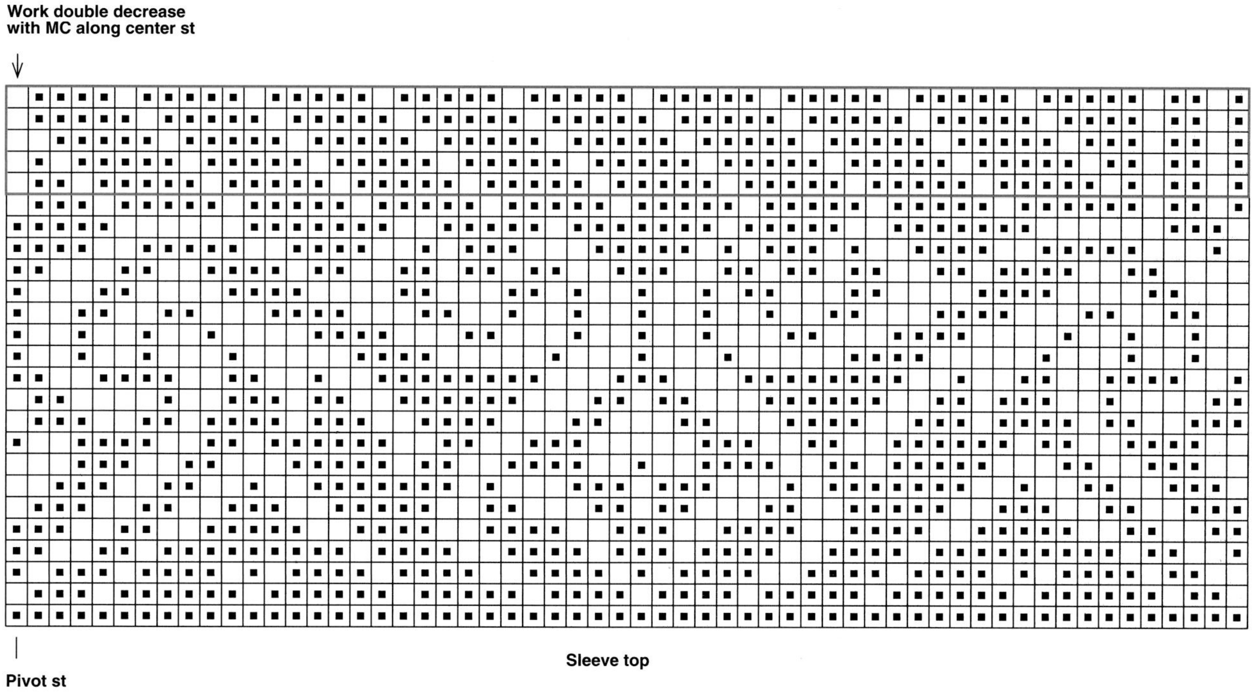

**Work double decrease
with MC along center st**

Sleeve top

Pivot st

Lupine Cardigan

THE LUPINE, MEDALLION, RAM'S HORN AND FAIR Isle Cardigans that follow are all basically identical in shape, modeled after the traditional Norwegian drop-shoulder style. The body (with steek allowance) is a tube knitted from the lower edge to the bottom of the neck opening, without a thought about armholes. A second steek is made for the neck and knitting continues to desired length to shoulder. The sleeves are worked from cuff to shoulder, the armholes machine-stitched and cut open and the sleeves are then knitted or sewn in. (There is a "new" machine-less crocheted steek to be considered as well—it is explained on page 23.) The steek at center front is stitched and cut, and stitches are knitted up along one side, around the neck, and down the other side. The entire border is then knitted directly onto the body in one piece.

Although all three garments have their basic construction in common, they differ in weight of wool, gauge, color patterns, lower edges, and border treatment.

The Lupine design was in direct response to a number of requests for more details on how to knit a cardigan in the round. This specific garment has the appeal of relative simplicity, the challenge of steeks, a small color pattern and all the technical details of a garter-stitch, one-piece border. It was designed for knitters to whom circular construction is new, but it is also an opportunity for experts to remember what pure, soothing pleasure it is to knit a stretch of plain stocking stitch.

There is a bit of shaping for the neck front, followed by a narrow band of color pattern across the top of the body and sleeves. The neck and sleeve shaping are designed to be completed before the color pattern begins, so you can concentrate upon one thing at a time.

The final border includes the appropriate knit-up ratio, mitered corners, back-of-neck shaping, buttonholes and 2-stitch I-cord casting off. Techniques are detailed on pages 12–24. I used Rangeley Wool—the medium weight and stunning colors are ideal for a cardigan. Ready?

Finished size

40 (42, 44)" (101.5 [106.5, 112] cm) chest circumference; about 27 (28, 28)" (68.5 [71, 71] cm) long.

Yarn

Rangeley wool (100% wool; 210 yd/4 oz): lupine (MC), 7 (8, 8) skeins; 2-ply Sheepswool (100% wool; 210 yd/4 oz): pale gray (CC), 1 skein.

Needles

Approximately size 7 (4.5 mm): 16" (40-cm), 24" (60-cm) and 40" (80-cm) circular and set of double-pointed for cuffs. Adjust needle size to obtain the correct gauge.

Notions

9 pewter buttons, about nickel-sized.

Gauge

18 sts = 4" (10 cm); 4 1/2 sts = 1" (2.5 cm).

Note: The circumference of the body at the widest point, times gauge, is considered 100%, or the key number [K] (See EPS, page 16). All other dimensions will be a percentage of [K].

Body: With MC and 24" (60-cm) needle, cast on 90% of [K] plus 5 extra "steek" sts for cutting later—163 + 5 (171 + 5, 179 + 5) sts. Keep the center 5 steek sts in plain stocking st throughout. Assign 1 st each side of the steek for a future knit-up st to be used when working the final border. Join, being careful not to twist sts and mark st #3 of the center 5 as the beg of the rnd. Work k1b, p1 ribbing, noting that 1/1 ribbing requires the body sts to be divisible by 2 plus 1 to assure a mirror image of ribs each side of the center front steek. Work ribbing until piece measures about 3" (7.5 cm). Inc on next rnd to 100% [K] as follows:

Small: k5, [M1, k9] 17 times, M1, k5—181 + 5 steek sts.

Medium: k5, [M1, k9] 9 times, [M1, k10] 8 times, M1, k5—189 + 5 steek sts.

Large: k5, [M1, k10] 17 times, M1, k4—197 + 5 steek sts.

Find the exact side "seam" sts (excluding the 5 center-front sts in your counting) and mark them with coil-less pins. These marked sts will become the armhole cutting sts. Sail straight up the body to within 4 to 5" (10 to 12.5 cm) of desired length to shoulder. *Optional:* Insert one set of short rows (page 22) across the back at about 5 to 6" (12.5 to 15 cm) from lower edge, to prevent the dreaded riding up. *Optional:* Work a phony seam in each side st (page 21). ***Shape scooped neck:*** When designing your own neck shape, decide how deep and how wide you want the finished opening to be, remembering to allow for the width of the final edging which will fill in the opening a bit. I figured my opening to be roughly 5" (12.5 cm) deep, 5" (12.5 cm) wide at the bottom, scooping out to 8" (20.5 cm) wide at the top, and allowing for a 1" (2.5-cm) fill-in. That is a fairly large scoop and I encourage you to adjust according to personal preference.

Therefore, at 5" (12.5 cm) below desired length to shoulder, end rnd 11 sts before the steek and place the next 27 sts on a piece of wool (11 sts to the right of the steek + 5 center steek sts + 11 sts to the left of the steek). Cast on 5 new steek sts and complete the rnd. Isolate a knit-up st each side of the steek sts, and shape the neck on either side by working ssk after the steek, knit around, k2tog before the steek, every rnd 7 times—another 3" (7.5 cm) worth of sts consumed. This shaping takes a little less than 2" (5 cm) of vertical length, so you have just enough room to work the color pattern chart shown here. In order for the patterns to align at the shoulders, center the pattern from center back out to armhole cutting sts, then mirror-image the patterns on the other side of the cutting sts. (See box at right.) Be sure to keep the knit-up st on each side of the steek in MC throughout. Also, knit the carried color in the middle st of the steek for a built-in basting line.

When you reach desired length to shoulder, put all
body sts onto a length of wool. You may cast off the
steek sts or half-weave them in later (see page 16).

If you have reduced the scoop-size of the neck
opening, you may find yourself beginning the color
pattern before the neck shaping is done.

Sleeves: With MC and dpn, cast on 20% of [K]—
36 (38, 40) sts. Join, being careful not to twist sts.
Work k1b, p1 rib until piece measures 2 to 3" (5 to
7.5 cm). (*Note:* For a cute detail, cast on using the
long-tail method [see page 14] and keep the pale
gray wool over your thumb and the Lupine over
your forefinger. This will give an extra end to darn
in, but yields a nice outline around the cuff.) For a
bloused sleeve, inc as follows:

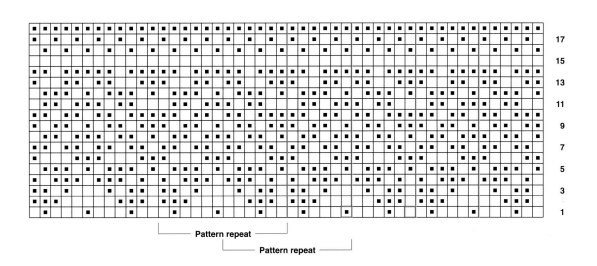

Pattern repeat

Pattern repeat

☐ main color

■ contrast color

☐ center pattern stitch

☐ center pattern stitch

Small: *K2, M1; rep from *—54 sts.

Medium: [K2, M1] 18 times, k2—56 sts.

Large: *K2, M1; rep from *—60 sts.

Work straight for about 5" (12.5 cm) changing to shorter needle when practical. Mark the 3 center underarm sts, and inc 2 sts every 4th rnd as follows: *Knit to marker, M1, k3 (marked sts), M1. Knit 3 rounds plain. Repeat from * until you have enough sts for the desired depth of your armhole (I inc'd to 88 sts)—nearly 10" (25.5 cm) deep.

You may be ready to begin the pattern now; if not, work straight to within 3" (7.5 cm) of desired total length. Knit the color pattern, centering it first, and cast off loosely. Casting off from the right side in purl using contrast color produces a pretty ridge. Knit another sleeve. (*Note:* For a standard, tapered sleeve, eliminate the severe inc above the ribbing and inc 1 st each side of centered 3 underarm sts every 4th rnd to desired width; then work straight to desired length.)

Finishing: *Machine stitching and cutting* With a blunt needle and CC, baste (if you haven't knitted-in your basting) down the center front neck steek. Using a small stitch and loose tension, machine stitch down one side of the basting, across the bottom, and up the other side. If this is your first time cutting, add a second reassuring line of stitching on top of the first. Stay as close to the center basting as possible (see page 20). Cut between the stitching lines, and watch the knitting fall open into a graceful curve. Now that the neck is open, you have greater access to baste and machine stitch the body, but do not cut the body open just yet—it is easier to sew in the sleeves without having the fronts flapping about.

To mark armhole depth, find the coil-less pins you put into the body "seam" sts so long ago and fold the body flat on a table. Place the sleeve along one side, matching center sleeve top with shoulder line, and mark on the "seam" st where the bottom of the sleeve hits the body. Run a basting thread from the shoulder down to that point; mark the other side to correspond. Machine stitch and cut as above.

In order to sew in the sleeve, you must first make an armhole by joining the shoulders. A firm seam is advised here to prevent the weight of the sleeve from dragging the shoulder down. I used 3-needle cast-off from the top side: Line up the front sts on a needle with the same number of back sts on

The 3-needle cast-off creates a beautiful ridged seam.

Sew the sleeve to the body with a blunt needle.

another needle not counting any raw steek sts. With a third needle, k2tog (the first st from each front and back needle), then *k2tog, pass last st over. Repeat from *. This is strongly related to regular old casting off, but you're knitting 2 sts tog each time. *For fussy knitters (FFK):* This beautiful ridged seam has a different appearance on each side. If you want the fronts to match, work the cast-off in the same direction. So, if you knitted the first seam from armhole to neck, work the second from neck to armhole. *Sew in sleeves:* Pin the center sleeve top to the shoulder seam and pin the underarm to the bottom of the armhole opening. Pin the halfway, then the quarter-way points. Sew the sleeve in from the "right" side, never veering from your chosen vertical sewing line on the body. Because the sts and rows do not match up in plain stocking st, do not bother counting them—simply dive in and out with the tapestry needle on the sleeve, then on the body. The pinned points will tell you when you have to slightly enlarge your bite on the body to keep it

For the garter-st border, knit up 2 sts for every 3 rnds of stocking st.

matched with the sleeve. **Garter-st border:** Cut the front open. Ah, a cardigan appears. Now, how many times have you seen a knitted cardigan with front borders that hang lower than the rest of the garment? Elizabeth and I call that "Dreaded Frontal Droop" (I thought that was much funnier when I was younger). To prevent DFD and allow for the 5-to-7 ratio of plain stocking st versus the perfect squareness of garter-st, Elizabeth discovered that knitting up 2 stitches for every 3 rounds of the body works beautifully.

With MC, 40" (80-cm) needle, and beg at the wearer's lower left corner, isolate the knit-up st and knit into rnds 1, 2, and skip rnd 3; knit up rnds 4, 5, and skip rnd 6. (*FFK:* When knitting up sts, you have four methods from which to choose. You may knit up the right half of the vertical st, the left half, both sides tog, or dive down through the middle of the st and hook the working wool up from below. The last method is always my choice when knitting up from a color pattern. However, on plain stocking st I like to go into the left half of the stitch, leaving

the right half to form a pretty little bead up the edge of the border. And by knitting up from the inside of the garment (wearer's left side) you produce purl bumps on the outside. This serves as the first ridge of the garter-st border and will lie snugly against the body. [If you began on the other side, there would be a stocking-st gap between body and border.])

Cont to knit up 2 sts for every 3 rnds into the same vertical st all the way to the neck corner. Slide the raw neck sts onto the other end of the working needle and knit them. Knit up 5 sts for the 7 dec rows of neck shaping, then go back to knitting up 2 sts for every 3 rnds through the color-pattern section (and rejoice that you left the knit-up unencumbered by color pattern). Work all sts across the back neck. *Note:* Because the body ends in CC and you are working from the "wrong" side, purl the MC sts across the neck-back on this initial pass. Now reverse the foregoing: Knit up 2 for 3 through pattern, 5 out of 7 around neck shaping, 1 for 1 across raw neck sts, and 2 for 3 down right front to lower edge. All edge sts are now securely on the needle, and you are poised to work the garter-st border. Turn. You are at the lower right corner, and will be knitting on the outside. I inserted a single CC ridge at this point, so join in the CC if you feel like it, and knit to the top right neck corner. **Mitered corners:** Mark the exact neck corner st on both right and left sides (flip a coin to decide whether it should be the final body st or the first horizontal neck st). *M1, k1 (corner st), M1, work to other corner; rep from *. This pair of incs is worked every other row

Mitered corners neatly finish the scooped neckline.

throughout the border, i.e., every outside row. Cont to lower left edge. Turn, and knit back plain. (*FFK:* Purl the 2 marked corner sts on every inside row if you wish the detail of a diagonal stocking-st line at each mitered corner.) Return to MC and, on the next ridge, dec across the neck back to prevent flaring as follows: Work to shoulder point, *k3, k2tog; rep from * across neck back sts to other shoulder point (don't mind if the rep doesn't come out evenly—you just want to get rid of about 6 to 7 sts), work to lower left edge. Cont back and forth on all sts, maintaining mitered corners. If you knit a wider border than I did, eliminate the final one or two increases.

Buttonholes: Thinking it a bit silly, I never much cared which gender required buttonholes on which side, and couldn't remember anyway. Juliet Crisp told me how to remember: *Women are always right.* I like the one-row buttonhole for the obvious reason that it is taken care of in one pass (see page 20). If you have a favorite buttonhole, by all means employ it here. I insert the buttonholes on the 3rd or 4th ridge, or near the halfway point on the border.

After a total of 6 or 7 ridges, never forgetting the mitered corners and the purl st on the inside, it is time to cast off. This is a critical part as you want neither a tight, pulled-up selvedge, nor a sloppy one. If you use regular old cast-off, I recommend working it from the right side in purl.

My current fave, Elizabeth's I-cord cast-off, takes a bit longer, but with great reward. I used 2-stitch I-cord as follows: Beg at lower right corner, make 2

backward loops (cord sts) on the end of the left needle. *K1, k2tog tbl (the last cord st, and 1 raw st-to-be-cast-off), replace 2 sts to left needle; rep from *. (*FFK:* Return 1 st to left needle, leave next st on right needle, insert tip of left needle into front of this st and knit. Yes, this results in a twisted st, but it is very tidy-looking, and you can zip along at great speed.)

Big excitement looms as you near the first mitered corner. It has looked rather puffy with all those incs, and now, as you nibble off the sts, you see the emergence of a perfectly snappy, right-angle corner. Cont along, firming your tension slightly as you work the front neck curves. If this had been a longer section, like a V-neck, I would have maintained the 2-for-3 pick-up ratio along the shaped section, but because it is only 7 rows high, I just skipped 2 sts. Darn in all ends. Wash and block (see page 24).

Finishing cut edges: If you heeded the words on page 20, and machine stitched into the left and right halves of the center steek st, you will have no short ends or tufts to deal with. Simply fold the half-steek flap toward the body, poke under only the half-st with the line of machine stitching through it, and tack it down with matching thread (or split off one ply of wool). This produces the tidiest appearance, with the least amount of bulk, that I know of. I'm not very fussy about the hidden armhole edges but cardigan fronts flap open and the inside will be clearly visible, so neatness counts. If you did not cast off the steek sts, you may half-weave the raw sts to the body.

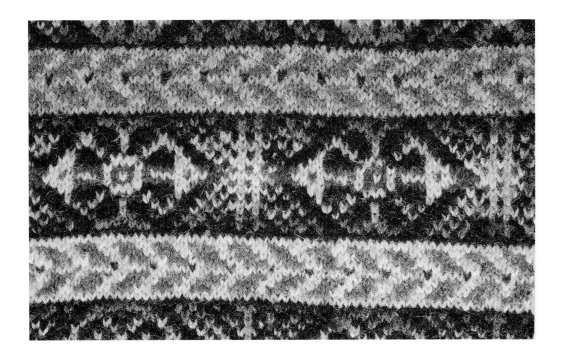

Fair Isle Cardigan

ON A SMALL ISLAND OFF THE NORTHERN TIP OF Door County, Wisconsin, and perched on the edge of the water, sits an ancient Icelandic square-hewn log cabin. Into this magical spot Chris and I settled ourselves for another knitting vacation. The Fair Isle project we worked on (me knitting and Camera Guy taping) was as deeply satisfying as the surroundings; "*. . . for always night and day / I hear lake water lapping with low sounds by the shore. . . .*" —William Butler Yeats, "The Lake Isle of Innisfree."

Those who have already experienced the excitement and contentment of knitting a true Fair Isle pattern need not be told of the pure pleasure involved. Elizabeth once described Fair Isle knitting as "painting with a different color in each hand and never having to rinse the brushes." For me it is like going into a trance. At first you must follow the chart slavishly, but soon you begin to see that even though the main pattern bands are different, they are the same; that the O and the X chase each other continuously but neither ever catches the other.

The rhythm of the chase becomes familiar even though the arrangement of the patterns changes. The "rules" for knitting in this traditional style add to its pleasure: Never carry more than two colors at a time and never strand a carry longer than an inch. The formerly-believed Fair Isle rule of "never purl back in color pattern" has been disproven by recent travelers to the Islands. Apparently the Shetland knitters are not of one mind on this subject. Some knit in the round to the armholes then switch to flat knitting for the front and back yokes; others cast on extra stitches at the underarms (a steek) to enable them to continue circular knitting and cut open the armholes and cardigan front; designers Lizbeth Upitis and Joyce Williams knit forwards and backwards from the underarm up—no steeks, no cutting, no purling back in pattern. Whichever method is used, the play of color is agreed upon: the color of the motif may shade from light to dark and back again, and the background color may shift at the same time. This can produce spectacular results even though only two colors are carried at a time.

It is this unique use of color that separates Fair Isle from other types of two-color work, and I think it a pity that the term "Fair Isle" has come to be applied to any color-pattern knitting, muddying the definition of what is a very succinct and specific type of pattern.

Chris and I had spent the month of March 1994 on a workshop tour of the West Coast with the landscape full of flowering trees and bulbs. Upon our return to Wisconsin in early April, everything looked somber and bleak by comparison. However, the subtle beauty of our northern pre-spring gradually made itself recognizable to my eye: I saw soft brown pine needles on the forest floor and the same color in last year's oak leaves which still clung to the branches; the freshly turned earth was a rich black/brown; there was light silver bark on the slim young maple trees, with the berries that precede their leaves a rich reddish brown; last year's meadow grasses had dried and turned flaxen, as had the corn stalks left to winter-over in the fields; the white pines were still pale and rather dusty before they got excited about spring and changed into their bright, shiny green. Those were the colors I could see from my knitting chair and those were the shades I drew from Schoolhouse's extensive Shetland wool palette: moorit, natural black, oatmeal, heather, honey beige, and ghillie green.

The construction details for this sweater are the same as for the Lupine Cardigan on pages 66–72. The two sweaters differ in gauge, charts, and the cardigan border treatment and gussets. Also, here the sleeves are knitted into the body instead of being sewn. To alter the size, use partial mirror-image repeats on either side of the center front. Shorten the body by eliminating the bottom peerie or an OXO. Or cast on invisibly and add corrugated rib last, adjusting to desired length.

Finished size

48" (122 cm) chest circumference; 28" (71 cm) long.

Yarn

Shetland wool (100% wool; 150 yd/oz): natural black, 6 oz; honey beige, heather, oatmeal, 3 oz each; moorit, ghillie green, 2 oz each.

Needles

Approximately size 4 (3.5 mm): 16" (40-cm), 24" (60-cm), and 40" (80 cm) circular (cir) and set of double-pointed (dpn). One size smaller 24" (60-cm) for the corrugated ribbing.

Notions

10 deer horn buttons, about nickel-sized.

Gauge

27 sts and 30 rows = 4" (10 cm); 6¾ sts and 7½ rows = 1" (2.5 cm).

I knitted, rather than purled, the last 7 rnds of heather in the ribbing.

Body: With heather and smaller 24" (60-cm) needle, cast on 280 sts + 7 center-front steek sts + 2 "balance" sts (see page 12)—289 sts total. Join, being careful not to twist sts. Work k2, p2 corrugated rib according to chart. Change to larger needle and work 1 plain rnd, following chart for your chosen length, and inc to 320 sts (100% [K] [see EPS, page 16]) as foll: *K7, M1; rep from * around

Continue with Chart 2

Fair Isle Chart 1

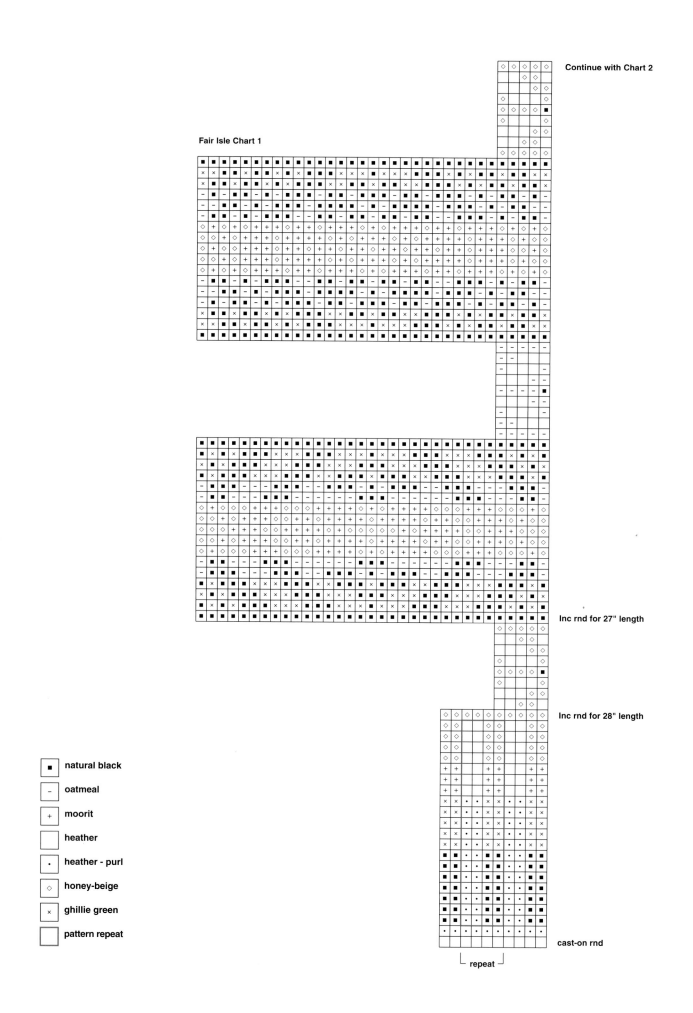

Inc rnd for 27" length

Inc rnd for 28" length

- ■ natural black
- − oatmeal
- + moorit
-   heather
- • heather - purl
- ◇ honey-beige
- × ghillie green
-   pattern repeat

cast-on rnd

└ repeat ┘

Fair Isle Chart 2

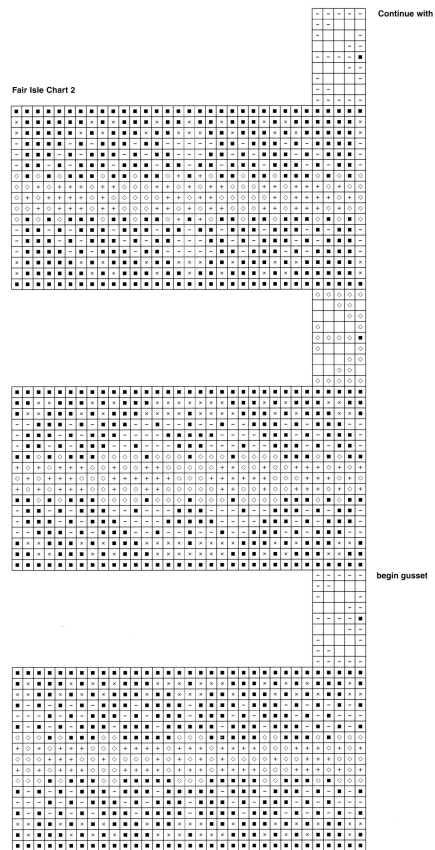

begin gusset

(not increasing in the center steek sts) + 7 steek + 1 "balance" st—328 sts total. Work color patt until piece measures 4" (10 cm) less than desired length to underarm. *Gussets:* Mark side "seam" sts and inc 1 st each side of marker every 4th rnd 7 times, working new sts in vertical stripes—15 gusset sts. Place gusset sts on holders and cast on 7 steek sts in their place. Cont working in the rnd until piece measures 4" (10 cm) less than desired shoulder height. For a scooped neck, place center 32 sts + 7 steek sts on holder and cast on 7 new steek sts in their place. Keeping one stitch in plain background color each side of steek (these will be your knit-up stitches for the border), dec 1 st each side of center steek 9 times. Work straight to desired height. Knit 1 final rnd in natural black (casting off steek sts, if desired) and place all sts on a thread.

Sleeve increases are worked in the appropriate background color.

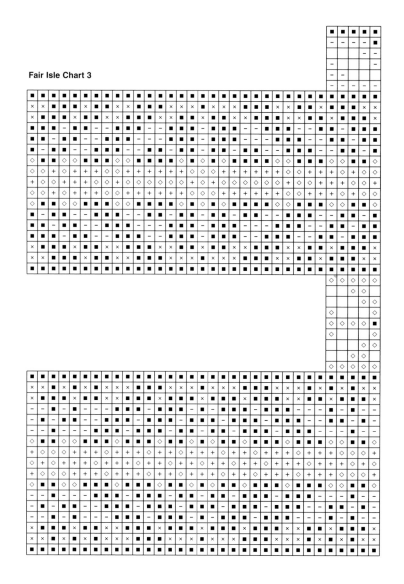

Fair Isle Chart 3

Sleeve: With heather and dpn, cast on 20% of body sts—64 sts. Join, being careful not to twist sts, place marker. Work corrugated rib. Work 1 rnd plain, inc as foll: K1, M1, *k2, M1; rep from * to last st, k1, M1—96 sts and 1 "balance" st—97 sts. Mark 3 center underarm sts. Cont in patt, inc 1 st each side of 3 marked sts as needed to get to upper arm measurement. (I needed 19 pairs of incs before the gusset and had 105 rnds in which to work, so I increased 2 sts every 5th rnd.) Continue until sleeve measures 4" (10 cm) less than total desired length. **Gussets:** Work gusset as for body (I ended up with 149 sts total.) Leave sts on needle. Machine stitch and cut all steeks (see page 20). From right side, join shoulders with 3-needle cast-off (see page 15). **Knit sleeves into armholes:** With natural black, knit up 144 sts around armhole, or number of sts to match *your* final sleeve sts. Beginning at center underarm, join to 144 sleeve sts by 3-needle cast-off from right side, as on shoulder.

Finishing: *Border* I tried three different versions before settling on a peerie-patterned band. Since this means stocking st attached to stocking st, and because the st and row gauges are practically square to each other, the pick-up ratio is 1-for-1, or possibly 10 sts for every 11 rnds (to suck it in a little bit and prevent the Dreaded Frontal Droop; see page 15).

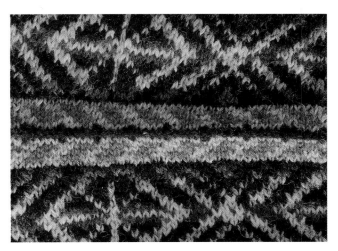

Join shoulders with the 3-needle cast-off from the right side.

Establish the peerie patt, reversing the direction of the peeries by mirror-imaging them at the upper, mitered, corners and again at the center back. One-row buttonholes (see page 20) fit neatly into the plain row in the center of the peerie. Note that the black st in the center row of the peerie pattern is missing in the buttonhole band—it's easier to work buttonholes in a solid color. At the end of the peerie, knit 1 row, purl 1 row in natural black and knit a facing that matches the buttonhole in honey beige. I admit that I found knitting back backward (see page 19) tedious and I worked garter st for the last 6 rows (3 ridges), ending with 1 row of natural black and casting off. My rationalization was that I was preventing the facing edge from curling and giving me trouble when I tacked it into place at the end. Ahhh. Weave in loose ends. Block. Sew on buttons.

Gussets are worked in vertical stripes.

I knitted the facing in honey beige to match the buttonholes.

Medallion Cardigan

I CALL THIS MY LILLEHAMMER SWEATER BECAUSE I planned to knit it during the 1994 Winter Olympics in Norway. As the starting date approached, I plotted the design and chose the wool. Once I had made the decisions, I was anxious to begin and actually finished the entire garment before the opening ceremonies. While watching the Olympics I paid particular attention whenever the cameras scanned the crowd, and I felt validated and prophetic as I noticed that many of the beautiful sweaters were black and white with red trim.

The basic construction of this jacket is identical to the preceding Lupine cardigan. The variations include corrugated ribbing, allover patterning, side panels, and triple I-cord edging on fronts and neck.

Finished size

47" (119.5 cm) chest circumference; 33" (84 cm) long.

Yarn

Québécoise wool (100% wool; 210 yd/3½ oz): black, 5 skeins; white (or cream), 4 skeins; red, 1 skein.

Needles

Approximately size 6 (4 mm): 16" (40-cm), 24" (60-cm) and 40" (80-cm) circular and set of double-pointed for cuffs. Adjust needle size to obtain the correct gauge.

Notions

Eight Norwegian pewter clasps or pewter buttons.

Gauge

22 sts and 24 rows = 4" (10 cm); 5½ sts and 6 rows = 1" (2.5 cm).

To adjust the circumference, add or subtract partial medallions. For different lengths, play with repeats of the three shaded disks shown in the chart. After a deep corrugated rib, the jacket shown has 3½ of the darkest disks, 3 of the medium, and 2½ of the palest. Bright red trims the sleeves, shoulders, and lower edges of cuffs and body. The triple layered I-cord edging in black, white, and red serves as the cardigan border. Norwegian pewter clasps add the final touch. If you'd rather have buttons, work Elizabeth's hidden I-cord buttonholes (see page 18) between two layers of the triple I-cord.

Body: Establish [K] (see EPS, page 16) by multiplying *your* gauge times your wanted circumference. Because corrugated ribbing has a tendency to roll if the long-tail method is used for casting on, use either the knitted-on or the German twisted method (see page 13) to cast on to help obviate that

tendency. With red and 24" (60-cm) needle, cast on 90% of [K]. Work 1 rnd *k1 white, p1 red; rep from *. Then work *p1 white, k1 black; rep from * for remainder of ribbing. Because purling is not my favorite stitch, after 2" (5 cm) I changed to *k1 white, k1 black; rep from * for the next 2" (5 cm)—it makes a nice change of texture. I staggered the top of the stripes by working the final rnd *k1 white, k3 black; rep from *. The side panels are started right after the cast on and the purl sts are marked on the chart.

Work 1 plain rnd black, inc up to [K] (do not increase through the side panels). Follow the chart. The neck shaping will differ slightly from the Lupine Cardigan because of the color pattern. When you are ready to begin neck shaping, knit to

After 2" of rib I changed from k1 black, p1 white to k1 black, k1 white.

The side panels begin immediately after the cast-on edge and interrupt the corrugated ribbing.

Medallion Body

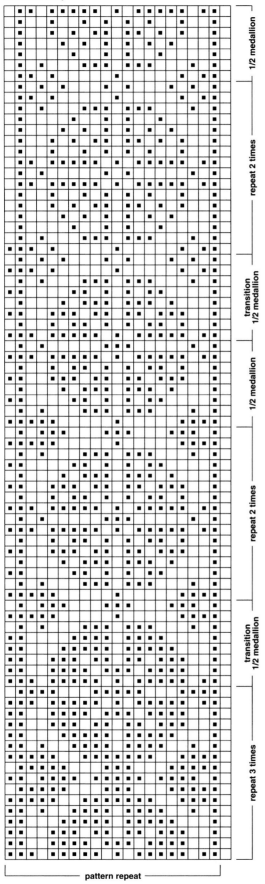

1/2 medallion

repeat 2 times

transition
1/2 medallion

1/2 medallion

repeat 2 times

transition
1/2 medallion

repeat 3 times

pattern repeat

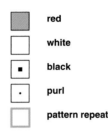

red

white

■ black

· purl

pattern repeat

Medallion Ribbing

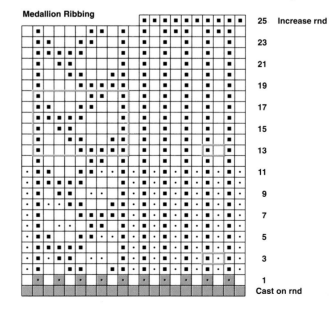

25   Increase rnd
23
21
19
17
15
13
11
9
7
5
3
1
Cast on rnd

the middle of the steek and break the yarn. Place the desired number of lower-neck sts on a thread, join in the working yarn at the right side of the neck opening, and cont in patt. When you arrive back at the center, cast on 5 new steek sts (keeping them in speckles) and establish 1 solid background-color knit-up st each side of the 5 steek sts. Shape neck by dec 1 st each side of the new steek until opening is desired width, then continue straight to shoulder. Knit the final rnd with red.

Knit sleeves as for the Lupine Cardigan, either tapered or bloused, or a combination thereof; measure, stitch, and cut armholes and center front.

The shoulders are joined by 3-needle, 2-stitch I-cord cast-off (see page 15), in red, beginning at the neck and working out to the shoulders. The sleeves are knitted into the armholes in a similar manner.

Join shoulders with 2-st I-cord cast off in red.

The sleeves were knitted in in red.

Triple applied 3-st I-cord border: *First layer:* With black, cast on 3 sts onto dpn and work attached I-cord, (see page 18) knitting the I-cord onto 9 sts for every 10 rows. This may vary for you. Employ the empirical method as follows: After 6 to 8" (15 to 20.5 cm), give the I-cord edging a yank and a judicious look. Is the I-cord pulling up? Is it too sloppy? Is it just right? Once the ratio has been established, cont up the front in that mode. At the corner, work one round of unattached I-cord before and after the attached corner st (to provide enough fabric to swing around that 90-degree turn), then apply to every st across the horizontal plane of the neck, working 2 raw sts tog a few times to prevent flaring. Attach 9 sts for every 10 rows up the side of the neck, dec across the neck back by working 2 tog every 5th or 6th st (eliminating about 5 to 7 sts total), 9 for 10 down other side of neck, nearly all sts on the horizontal plane, and 9 for 10 down the other vertical edge. Run the working wool through the final 3 sts, pull tight, and darn the end through the cord tube. *Second layer:* With a smaller needle and white, pick up **every** st (the ratio has already

As I PLOTTED THE DESIGN, I WANTED THE wide side panel to begin right away at the lower edge, in the middle of the corrugated rib. Because of the width of the panel, I worried that the stocking stitch would curl at the lower edge. I experimented with working purl stitches whenever I "could." When you purl a white stitch into a black stitch, it pulls black up into the white row and makes a blip. This is a beautiful design feature in Bohus knitting but, in my opinion, should be used judiciously in other areas. In this instance, when there was a white stitch above a white stitch I could purl it without producing a blip, and the purl stitches countered the curl of stocking stitch. I call this Purl When You Can (or PWYC) and it was my initial experimentation with this technique. You will find further use of it in other sweaters in this book (Turkish Maple, Turkish Ocean, Celtic Swirl, and Weeping Sun/Moon.)

This cuff is an example of my PWYC method.

been established) from the first layer, about 20 to 30 sts at a time and work another layer of attached I-cord. Because applying I-cord in a strongly contrasting color causes blips of the previous color to show through on the side that faces you as you work, I used to apply the cord to the "wrong" side of the garment and not worry about the blips. But now, thanks to designer Joyce Williams, we can defeat the blip. With the picked-up sts on the left needle and cord sts on the right needle, for a 3-st I-cord: *Replace the 3 cord sts to left needle, k2, sl 1, yo, k1 picked-up st, p2so (the slipped st and the yo). Rep from *. Lovely, huh? The yo acts as an outline st that covers the blip. ***Third layer:*** With red, apply another I-cord as before. To turn the top corners in I-cord, work one round of unattached cord before and after the actual corner st to provide extra fabric to swing around the turn.

You may want to insert hidden I-cord buttonholes (see page 18) in the second layer of cord, just in case you ever change your mind and want buttons on your jacket instead of clasps.

Ram's Horn Cardigan

THIS WAS MY FIRST VENTURE (ABOUT TEN OR twelve years ago) into Turkish color-pattern knitting, inspired by the book *Anatolian Knitting Designs* by Betsey Harrell. I remain fascinated by these designs, particularly the diagonal ones.

Have you noticed the "songs" that are hidden within nearly all stranded color patterns? They do not reveal themselves until you are actually knitting and have more or less familiarized yourself with the chart. It is the particular songs veiled within Turkish patterns that seem to have the most mysterious mathematical arrangements—simple, small-number repeats build to most complex-looking finished patterns and intriguingly rhythmical chants. It is almost like a secret code. Chris and I often discussed the possibility of musically scoring some of the knitting patterns.

Using two-ply (two strands of) unspun Icelandic wool turns this cardigan into a jacket by dint of the double-thick fabric produced by an allover pattern. With the addition of a scarf and mittens, I have often worn this sweater as a coat, which led me to

knit several knee-length, hooded Turkish coats. (One is in the book, *Knitting Around the World*, Taunton Press, 1993.)

A word about unspun Icelandic wool: I love this stuff. With it I have knitted traditional Swedish caps (called *Dubbelmössas*) in 1-ply at a gauge of 7 sts to 1" (2.5 cm), 1-ply lace shawls on size 10½ (6.5 mm) needles at a gauge of about 2 sts to 1" (2.5 cm), many 2-ply sweaters, jackets, and coats, and a 4-ply blanket. Technically, the form Schoolhouse Press imports from Iceland is a roving—the fibers have been carded and drawn out, but the fleece of the Icelandic sheep is so extraordinarily long that you may knit with the wool in this unspun state. It comes in small wheels (also called plates or cheeses) and you can knit 1-ply with the strand that comes from the center, or 2-ply with the center and outside strands together, or 3- or 4-ply from two wheels side by side. When you're traveling, it is easier to wind multiple plies together into balls first. You may also blend colors easily when knitting in 2-ply by working transition rounds with one strand

each of two colors. Unique to the unspun Icelandic wool is the ease with which you can spit-splice. Simply draw out the last few inches of the end of one wheel and the first few inches of the new wheel. Overlap the two ends on your palm. "Moisten" the other palm and rub them together briskly for five seconds. The combination of heat and damp will fuse the ends and because you d-r-e-w out the wool first, you will have no discernable thickening. *And warm? Uff!* Because the wool is unspun, many guard hairs stick out and create a haze over the surface of the fabric. This woolly aura is exceedingly efficient at trapping body heat. Within half a minute of flinging a 1-ply unspun Icelandic lace shawl over your shoulders, you can feel a marked rise in temperature.

Using the same basic construction as the Lupine Cardigan (see pages 66-72), establish your gauge, work your calculations, and follow the chart, enlarging or reducing the circumference by adding or subtracting half or full pattern repeats, or vertical lines at the side "seams." The main difference from the Lupine cardigan is the allover color pattern and the use of hems at the lower edge of the body and cuffs on the brown model, and corrugated cuffs and hem on the gray model.

The Ram's Horn chart is an 18-stitch repeat, but you can work in increments of 9 stitches as long as you center the 18-stitch pattern fore and aft. I have half-patterns at each side on the gray version, separated by vertical stripes. You may enlarge or reduce the number of stripes to alter the size slightly, or add or subtract units of 9 stitches for a greater alteration.

Finished size

The gray version is 46" (117 cm) around and 31" (79 cm) long. (Actually, the gray version measures 45" [114.5 cm] around lower edge, and by switching to a larger size needle near waist length, is 46" [117 cm] around chest. Knitter's choice.)

Yarn

Unspun Icelandic wool (100% wool; 300 yd/3½ oz) worked 2-ply (doubled): cream and silver gray, 4

wheels each; blacksheep, 2 wheels; steel gray, 1 wheel. Or play with brown variations: blacksheep, dark caramel, caramel, and beige.

Needles

Approximately size 8 (5 mm): 16"and 40" (40- and 80-cm) circulars and set of double-pointed (if you choose corrugated cuffs).

Notions

9 buttons of your choice. (On the gray version I used turquoise and silver—both faux—a bit larger than nickel-sized. For the brown model, I used Norwegian pewter clasps.)

Gauge

17 sts and 17 rows = 4" (10 cm); 4¼ sts and 4¼ rows = 1" (2.5 cm).

Shading: Use one strand of each of two shades for 3 rounds (see chart).

With Blacksheep, the 40" needle, and using the long-tail method (see page 14), cast on 193 + 5 sts. Designate the center 5 sts as steek sts plus a knit-up st each side of the steek, leaving 191 sts for patterning. Consider the outline-st side of long-tail cast-on to be the "right" side (see page 21) and, with the center of the steek as your starting point, join, being sure not to twist sts on needle. Beg the chart right

Corrugated ribbing for cuff (optional)

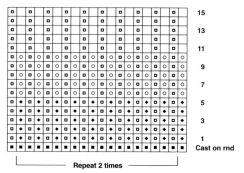

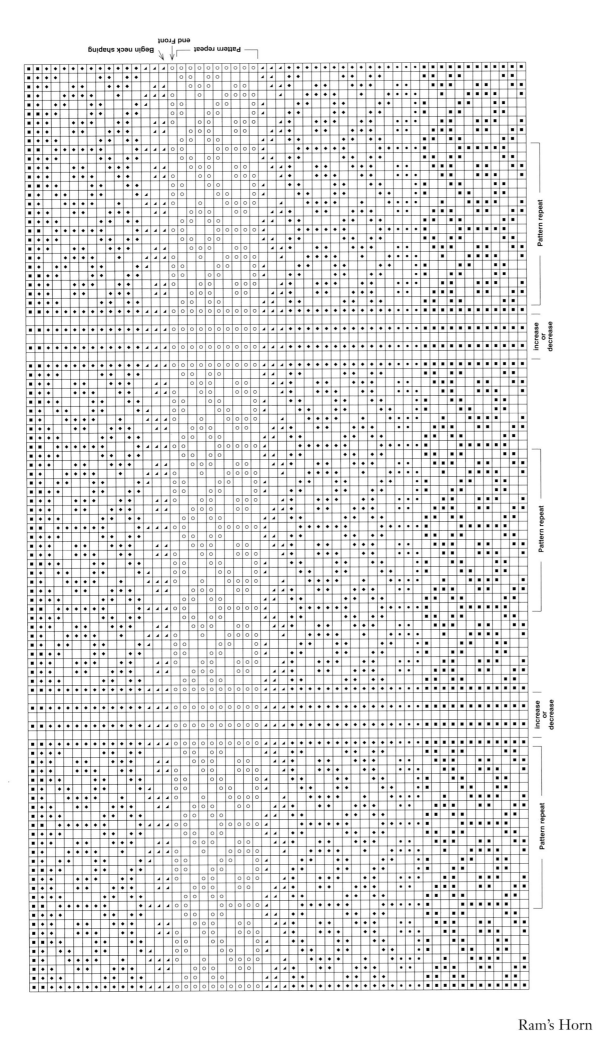

Begin neck shaping
end Front
Pattern repeat

CC1

CC2

CC2 + CC3

CC2

CC3 + CC4

CC3

CC4

purl with CC2

Ram's Horn Cardigan   89

away (I'll deal with the hem later on), keeping steek sts in alternate speckles and knit-up edge sts in working contrast color throughout. Work to about 4" (10 cm) from desired length to shoulder. **Shape neck:** Knit to the middle of the steek. Place the center 35 sts on a holder—15 left front + 5 steek + 15 right front sts. Alas, because this cardigan has a color pattern, here you must break the yarn (not

necessary in the plain knit Lupine jacket). Join them in again at the left edge and cont around in pattern. When you arrive back at the center, cast on 5 new steek sts (keeping them in speckles) and establish 1 solid background-color knit-up st each side of the 5 steek sts. Dec 1 st each side of the new steek 6 times as follows: ssk on the left side, and k2tog on the right side. Then cont straight to end of chart.

Ram's Horn Sleeve

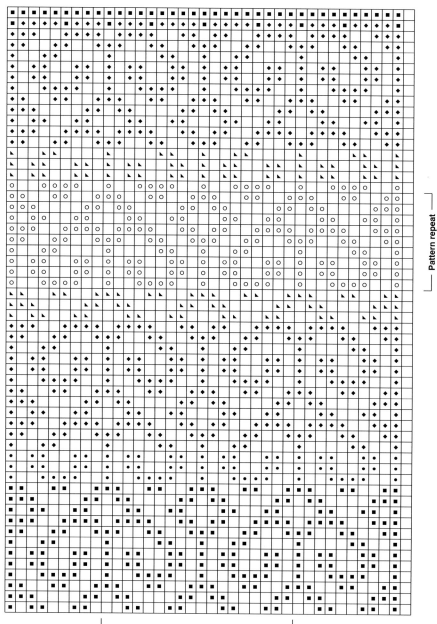

Pattern repeat

Repeat 2 times

Corrugated rib looks great in this subtly shaded Icelandic wool.

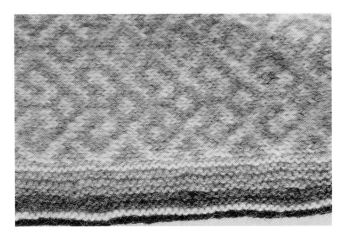

Work a garter-st border in stripes if you want.

Sleeves: With double-pointed needles (or 2 circulars; see page 20), cast on 38 sts. Work corrugated ribbing for about 3" (7.5 cm), shading colors as indicated on cuff chart. Inc evenly to 56 sts. The brown model has a wide, hemmed cuff which begins with 56 sts. I knitted the sleeve straight and increased for a half-gusset near the top.

Sleeve Shaping: After working the charted pattern for 4 to 5" (10 to 12.5 cm), inc 1 st each side of the 3 underarm sts every 5th rnd until sleeve is as wide as you want it (mine is 88 sts around). Work chart for 19" (48.5 cm). Keep the inc'd sts in vertical stripes or incorporate them into the color pattern as they appear. Knitter's choice.

Stitch and cut as for Lupine Cardigan. Unite shoulders. Sew or knit in sleeves. Knit up and work garter-st border as on page 71, adding garter-st stripes of the other colors if you want.

Finishing: *Body and cuff hems:* I think hems are not widely used because, if not properly executed, they look rather sad—they can cause the lower edge of the body to flare out and may form a dimpling horizontal line where the hem is joined to the body. Hems also may be thick and klutzy looking. These problems can all be solved. (See pages 16–17 for discussion of hems.)

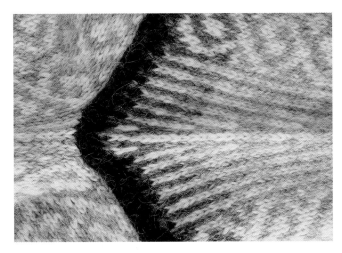

I kept my sleeve increases in stripes.

The inside hem is a perfect place to personalize your sweaters.

Saddle-Sleeved Jackets

CHRIS AND I TOOK A KNITTING VACATION through the magnificent Blue Ridge Mountains of Virginia, North Carolina, and Tennessee, videotaping and knitting a Bavarian twisted-stitch V-neck cardigan as we went. A traditional garment of this type usually has nary a plain knitted stitch in it but, instead, purls, twisted knits, traveling stitches, and perhaps cables. This produces a very handsome and impressive result, but it is a long, slow process, which meant I was unable to finish the garment by the end of the vacation. As with most of my designs, this one changed from my original concept as I worked, and I found myself knitting a rather interesting garter stitch shoulder-and-sleeve saddle. After I finished the Bavarian version, I liked the construction so well that I made several plain models for those who may not want to launch into the time-consuming twisted-stitch version.

The design produces a jacket with deeply inset (kangaroo pouch) armholes, worked in the round from lower edge to within about three or four inches of desired length to shoulder. The armholes and center front are stitched and cut, and the deep garter-stitch saddle is worked from the center neck back to each cuff, knitted onto the garment as you go for no-sew throughout. You may shape the body for a belted waist, or not. You may inset the armholes to set-in-sleeve width (with sleeve-cap shaping) or make a semi-dropped shoulder. You may run a cable or lines of phony seams through the garter-stitch section, or not. You may knit on a shallow or a deep shawl collar, or not. You may make a pullover instead of a cardigan. As usual, knitter's choices abound.

The fairly complex Bavarian twisted stitch version is worked in Québécoise because you need a firmly-spun wool to achieve the carved-in-wool sculpted effect of this type of texture knitting.

I chose unspun Icelandic wool to knit the plain jackets because this luxurious hairy wool is amazingly warm yet lightweight. Just what I want. I'll give you instructions for the plain one first.

Note: This circular jacket has an allowance of 5 extra "steek" stitches at the center front for the cardigan cutting and facing. I wanted a hem at the

lower edge, so I used a long-tail cast-on to facilitate this (see page 14). You may certainly substitute ribbing or garter stitch at the lower edge if you like.

Finished size

40 (44, 48, 52)" (101.5 [112, 122, 132] cm) chest circumference. Total length is up to you: about 26 (27, 28, 28)" (66 [68.5, 71, 71] cm) for a cardigan; about 2" (5 cm) longer for a jacket. Armhole depth is 9 (10, 10, 11)" (23 [25.5, 25.5, 28] cm).

Yarn

Unspun Icelandic wool (100% wool; 300 yd/3.5 oz) worked 2-ply (doubled): 7 (8, 9, 10) wheels. The two versions shown here are in natural shades of beige and palest gray.

Needles

Approximately size 8 (5 mm): 24" or 29" (60 cm) or 40" (80 cm).

Notions

I didn't use any, but you may want buttons.

Gauge

3.75 sts = 1" (2.5 cm).

Pulling one strand from the inside, and one from the outside of the "wheel" of wool for 2-ply, and using the long-tail method if you want a hem, cast on 150 + 5 sts for the center steek, (165 + 5, 180 + 5, 195 + 5) sts. Join, being careful not to twist sts. Knit around, marking the side "seam" sts with coil-less pins for any future shaping you may wish to do (see "Jacket Embellishments" ahead). Cont until piece measures 17 (18, 18, 19)" (43 [46, 46, 48.5] cm) from beg. *V-neck shaping:* (You decide where you want the V-neck to beg in relationship to the armholes and the lower edge.) Dec 1 st each side of center 5 steek sts as follows: *Knit the steek sts, ssk, knit around to within 2 sts of steek, k2tog. Knit 3 rnds plain. Rep

from * 8 times, and *at the same time*, when piece measures 17 (17, 18, 18)" (43 [43, 46, 46] cm) from beg, or desired length to underarm *shape kangaroo pouch armholes:* Place 23 (29, 37, 45) sts on threads at each underarm, centered above "seam" st on each side. (Note: This allows for a 14" [35.5-cm] shoulder-to-shoulder width; adjust this number to suit your desired shoulder width for a set-in sleeve or a semi-dropped-shoulder style.) Cast on 5 steek st in their place, and cont around, maintaining V-neck shaping at center front. When armholes measure 6½ (7, 7, 7)" (16.5 [18, 18, 18] cm), place all sts on a holder.

Cut steeks: Baste down the centers of the 3 steeks. Machine stitch (using small stitches and loose tension) down the left side of the center steek sts and up the right side of the same st. Cut open just one armhole and the V-neck. Don't cut all the way to the bottom of the body as it is easier to knit the sleeves without the body flapping about.

Right Yoke/Sleeve (wearer's right): At center back, use the invisible method (see page 13) to cast on 10 (10, 10, 13) sts. Work back and forth in garter st (perpendicular to the body), joining the last st of every other row to the raw body sts as follows: *K9 (9, 9, 12), yarn fwd, sl 2 sts pwise (the last yoke st and 1 raw body st), turn, k2tog, k to end, turn; rep from * until you are even with the front neck edge, then invisibly cast on 13 (13, 13, 16) more sts—23 (23, 23, 29) cast-on sts total. Mark the center of these sts for a phony seam (see Jacket Embellishments ahead). See how the neck back is lowered slightly? Cont to join sts on the back as established, but on the front, work to last st, ssk (last yoke st and 1 raw front body st), turn, yarn fwd, sl 1 st pwise. These two methods of joining sts will be reversed when you work the left half of the saddle sleeve to produce a handsome, matching stocking-st line at each of the four joins, so stay alert.

When you reach the armhole edge, pick up 2 sts for every 3 rnds on cut armhole selvedges and all the raw sts at underarm. Now, either work sleeve-cap shaping (see Jacket Embellishments ahead), or ignore sleeve-cap shaping and knit back and forth on all vertical sleeve sts, joining the end st of each row to a raw kangaroo-pouch st as you did on the shoulders, until all pouch sts are gone. And *at the same time*, beg dec at center top of sleeve when you reach the armhole edge. Mark the 12 (12, 12, 15)th st and from the "right" side, *k2tog, knit marked st, ssk. Knit 6 ridges (12 rows) plain. Repeat from * every 7th ridge about 4 or 5 times. Work straight to just above elbow length and switch the dec to the underarm, 1 or 2 sts in from each selvedge every 5th or 6th ridge, or even faster (depending on desired circumference at cuff and length in which to get there; I worked to 20" [51 cm] from inset armhole to cuff and ended up with 39 sts). Use Elizabeth's I-cord cast-off as follows: On left needle, cast on 2 cord sts. *K1, k2tog tbl (last cord st and 1 st to be cast off), replace 2 sts to left needle; rep from * around cuff. Now you may either sew up the sleeve seam **or** work 3-needle I-cord cast-off (see page 15) for a most satisfying and handsome method of joining the seam without sewing that mirrors the phony seams on the sleeves.

I worked a pair of single decs as above at the sleeve top instead of a double dec so I could insert a phony seam (see page 21) between them. Then I thought it a shame to end the beautiful horizontal line of stocking st that was produced when the saddle was joined to the raw underarm sts, so I added two more phony seams at those points.

By beg the sleeve dec at the center top, you will produce a more anatomical shape. Then switching to the underarm at the half-way point will prevent the decs from chewing up the phony seams.

Left Yoke/Sleeve: Pick up the 10 (10, 10, 13) sts from the invisible cast-on at center back neck, and work as for right yoke/sleeve, remembering to reverse the method of joining the yoke to the raw body sts. As you peruse this, it may seem complicated, but when you are there, you will be able to *read* your knitting and it should all make sense.

Finishing: *Hem* With single strand of yarn and working from behind the outline st (see page 21) of long-tail cast-on, knit up 1 st for every cast-on st around the lower edge except the steek sts. Knit 10

to 12 rnds, and work a wrapped steek at center front as follows: Wrap the yarn around the right needle 9 times, then cont knitting. When you get back there on the next rnd, remove the 9 loops and wrap 9 times afresh. Work to desired hem depth. Cut the center front open bet the machine stitching. Snug up each of the long wrap-ladders and cut through the middle. Skim each end lightly to the inside of the hem. Sew the raw hem sts down right off the needle (twisting the unspun yarn in the sharp sewing-up needle as you go). ***Plain cardigan border:*** Beg at lower left side, knit up 2 sts for every 3 rnds to the V-neck. Knit up 4 sts for every 5 rnds on the diagonal slope. Remove waste yarn from the invisible cast-on at front neck edge. You may (or

Knit up 2 sts for every 3 rnds up center front for a garter-st border. Knit up 4 sts for 5 rnds at the diagonal slope.

may not!) now need to rip back 1 row of the yoke to keep the continuity of garter st as you knit across the yoke. Knit up 1 st for each ridge across the back neck, and mirror-image down the right side. Turn. Knit back and forth for 6 to 8 ridges, adding your favorite buttonholes on the appropriate side after 3 or 4 ridges. Work I-cord cast-off (see page 15). Or . . . ***Shallow shawl collar border:*** (See page 21 for short rows and wrapping technique.) Knit up all border sts as above (to lower right front), turn, knit to left shoulder top, wrap, turn, knit to right shoulder line, wrap, turn. *Knit to 3 sts past last turn, wrap, turn; rep from * until you reach the beg of the V-neck shaping (about 14 ridges at center back), or desired depth of collar. Knit on to the lower edge and work back and forth on *all* sts until the border is 6 to 8 ridges wide on lower section. Cast off (in contrasting color if desired). Or . . . ***Deeper shawl collar:*** Knit to 5 sts past center back neck st, wrap, turn, knit to 5 sts past center back, wrap, turn. *Knit

I cast off the shawl collar in contrasting color.

to 3 sts past last turn, wrap, turn; rep from * to beg of V-neck shaping. If this is still not deep enough for you, knit *2* sts past last turn each time. You may insert as many garter-st ridges as you like—the collar depth is entirely up to you.

Jacket Embellishments

Back of body shaping: To avoid having the jacket ride up at the back, insert a set of short rows (see page 22) across the back only about 4" (10 cm) from lower edge.

Waist shaping: At about 5" (12.5 cm) before actual waistline, *knit to within 3 sts of marked "seam" st, k2tog, k3, ssk; rep from * for other side. Knit 2 rnds plain. Rep from * 3 or 4 times (depending on how much you want the waist to nip in)—12 or 16 sts eliminated. Knit 4 rnds plain at actual waist length. Now inc the 12 or 16 sts by working M1 each side of the 3 marked sts every 3rd rnd 3 or 4 times. If you need extra chest measurement, you may inc a few more times. By the same token, if you need greater hip measurement, don't inc all the way back to your original cast-on number.

Sleeve cap shaping: Knit to 5 sts past marked center-top sleeve st, wrap, turn, knit to 5 sts past center. Work back and forth, adding 5 sts more at each end 10 times (5 ridges). Knit the rest of the vertical sts and cont back and forth, consuming a kangaroo-pouch st at the end of each row, in the same manner that you joined the saddle to the body sts. (Omit the foregoing for a dropped shoulder.) If you have a particularly deep armhole, consider working decs at both center top and side selvedges as you knit toward the cuff.

Phony seam sleeve detail: A few inches past the armhole (with or without sleeve-cap shaping), drop the center top shoulder st back down to neck edge. With a crochet hook, hook up 2 ladders at a time. I also made a phony seam where the yoke joins the top of the body on both front and back. Do the phony seam every 4 to 5" (10 to 12.5 cm). With this hairy Icelandic wool, it is easier to drop stitches in short increments rather than work the entire length after the sleeve is finished.

Phony seams are an interesting finishing detail.

No-sew sleeve seam: Yes, it is a game of mine to eliminate sewing-up whenever possible, but this time it has a visual logic to it as well. Following the I-cord cast-off of the cuff sts, do not break the wool, but pick up 1 st for each ridge along the sleeve selvedges (a separate needle for each side) and hold them parallel to each other. To turn an I-cord corner, knit an extra round of the 2 cord sts from cuff cast-off. Then transfer them to one of the pick-up needles, and *k1, sl 1, k2tog (1 picked-up st from each selvedge), psso. Replace 2 cord sts on one of the pick-up needles. Rep from * along the seam. I call this 3-needle I-cord cast-off and it will more or less match the phony seams to augment the homogeneous appearance of the jacket. I find these small details enormously pleasing.

Reversible phony seam at collar edge: This may be worked through the garter-st border after the collar is finished, but before casting off. Drop the collar st that will meet the shoulder seam. See how the garter st separates into front and back ladders? (You can put your finger down the "tube" between them.) Grab the dropped st and, with a crochet hook, hook up each front ladder (in reality, every other st). Then, because you have already used the dropped st, twist a lose strand of wool into a st on the other side and hook up every other ladder.

I-cord cast off for cardigan border: Beg at lower corner, cast on 2 sts. *K1, k2tog tbl (2nd cord st and 1 raw st to be cast off), replace 2 sts to left needle; rep from *. If you are using a strongly contrasting color, use Joyce Williams's variation to defeat the blip as follows: *K1, sl 1, yo, k1, p2so (the slipped st and the yo), replace 2 sts; repeat from *.

Belt loops: From the fabric of the body, knit up 5 sts. Work back and forth in stocking st for about 12 rows. Weave raw sts to upper body. Rep at other side. The stocking-st selvedges will curl under obligingly and the finished loop will resemble a wide I-cord.

Elizabeth's I-cord belt: Cast on 10 sts. *K8, yarn fwd, sl 2 sts pwise, turn; rep from * ad infinitum. The belt may be narrowed or widened by varying the number of garter sts between the built-in I-cords at each selvedge; knitter's choice.

Bavarian Twist Saddle-Sleeved Cardigan

I WILL GIVE YOU THE NUMBERS FROM THE garment I knitted in the mountains, and trust that if you are experienced enough to launch into this beautiful type of texture knitting, you will also know how to alter the numbers to fit your gauge and measurements. Here is where my "bird's-eye-view" shown on page 102 is useful to redesign a garment; figure total number of stitches for the circumference you want, place the large motifs around the oval, add up the number of stitches they take, then fill in between them with purl, twisted knit, and perhaps 2-stitch cables to get to the desired number of stitches. I recommend that you use a firmly-twisted wool to show off the splendid sculptured effect to best advantage.

When I'm knitting cables and twisted stitches, I automatically mirror-image the patterns on either side of the center of a piece—I just read the same stitch chart backwards.

There are four methods of working each twisted travelling stitch. I recommend you practice each one and check the results against the ease of execution, then make your decision. Every time I say "knit," please understand that I mean "knit into the back of the stitch."

Right Twist Knit over Purl

1. Work the stitches out of order on left needle, knitting the second, then purling the first.

2. Take two stitches off left needle and reverse them, bringing the second stitch in front of the first and knitting it, then purling the next.

3. Transfer two stitches to right needle. With left needle, grab the purl stitch from behind and slide both stitches off right needle, letting the knit stitch fall free for a moment. Pick up the knit stitch and put it onto left needle and knit the first stitch, then purl the second.

4. Leave stitches on left needle. Grab the knit stitch from front and slide both stitches off left needle, letting the purl stitch fall free for a moment. Pick up the purl stitch with left needle, and insert left needle into the knit stitch and knit it, then purl the purl stitch.

I prefer the third method above the others. It becomes surprisingly smooth to execute after a bit of practice, and causes the least amount of stitch distortion.

Right Twist Knit over Knit

(Work as described above, substituting a knit stitch for the purl stitch.)

Left Twist Knit over Purl

1. Work stitches out of order on left needle (a bear, this one). Grab the second stitch from behind and purl it, then knit the first stitch and drop both from left needle.

2. Take the two stitches off the left needle, reverse them back onto left needle (ducking *under* the working wool and crossing the first [knit] stitch in front of the second [purl] stitch) and work.

3. Transfer both stitches to right needle. With left needle grab the knit stitch from in front and slide both stitches off right needle, letting the purl stitch fall free for a moment. Pick up the purl stitch from behind (and *under* working wool) with right needle, place on left needle and work.

4. Leave stitches on left needle. From *under* the working wool, grab the purl stitch from behind and slip both stitches off left needle. Pick up the knit stitch with left needle, slip the purl stitch to the left needle, and work the stitches.

Again, I prefer the third method.

Left Twist Knit over Knit

Work as described above, substituting a knit stitch for the purl stitch. Method 1 is not such a bear and methods 2, 3, and 4 do not require ducking under working wool.

Finished size

44" (112 cm) chest circumference; about 28" (71 cm) long.

Yarn

Québécoise wool (100% wool; 210 yd/3½ oz [100 g]): 10 skeins.

Needles

Approximately size 6: 24" or 29" (60-cm) and 40" (80-cm) circular. (Cable needle, optional.) Adjust needle size to obtain the correct gauge.

Gauge

22 sts = 4" (10 cm); 5½ sts = 1" (2.5 cm) in twisted-stitch pattern after blocking.

I cast on 216 + 7 steek sts around the lower edge, and established the patterns immediately. Each motif is originally separated by a p2, k2b, p2 "filler." I eliminated the need for a lower edge treatment by sneakily increasing 1 st into each purl section (except at center-front) after about 3 or 4" (7.5 to

10 cm). Thus I achieved my wanted body circumference (244 sts + 7) and had an organic, natural-born (as Pogo would say) ribbing. Continue as for the plain saddle shoulder cardigan (page 94) with kangaroo pouch armholes, V-neck shaping, machine stitching and cutting, and the garter-stitch yoke and sleeves.

I ran cable #155 (see chart) down the tops of the sleeves, decreasing each side of the cable (starting with the left half of the cable going toward the left sleeve and the right half of the cable going toward the right sleeve). I fussed about the relationship of

I ran a cable down the top of the sleeve, decreasing each side of it for shaping.

the garter-stitch sleeve to the cable. Although I did not come up with an actual formula, I found it necessary to work a short row each side of the cable every 10 rows (5th ridge) as follows: *Knit to cable, wrap, turn, knit back*. Knit across all sts and repeat from * to * on other side of cable. Since the cable is a 10-row repeat, it is easy to remember to insert the short rows every time you twist the cable. Without these inserted ridges, the cable bulged. You may decide to eliminate both the cable *and* the fuss and work plain sleeves with the handsome "phony seam" detail in lieu of a cable.

Here are the charts I used, taken from the trilogy of books by Maria Erlbacher, *Überlieferte Strickmuster*. The books are published by the museum of the Castle of Trautenfels, which is tucked away in a remote and romantic section of the Austrian Alps. The charts are traditional and authentic patterns of this region of Austria.

The cable along the top of the saddle continues down the sleeves.

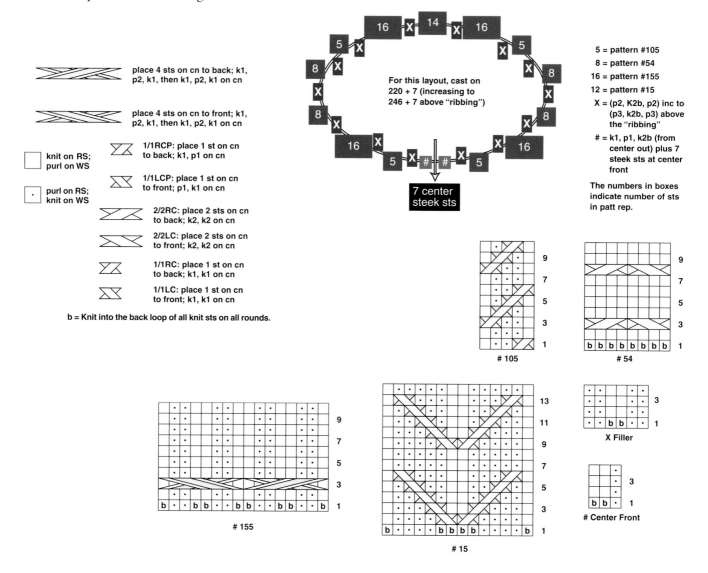

place 4 sts on cn to back; k1, p2, k1, then k1, p2, k1 on cn

place 4 sts on cn to front; k1, p2, k1, then k1, p2, k1 on cn

knit on RS; purl on WS

purl on RS; knit on WS

1/1RCP: place 1 st on cn to back; k1, p1 on cn

1/1LCP: place 1 st on cn to front; p1, k1 on cn

2/2RC: place 2 sts on cn to back; k2, k2 on cn

2/2LC: place 2 sts on cn to front; k2, k2 on cn

1/1RC: place 1 st on cn to back; k1, k1 on cn

1/1LC: place 1 st on cn to front; k1, k1 on cn

b = Knit into the back loop of all knit sts on all rounds.

For this layout, cast on 220 + 7 (increasing to 246 + 7 above "ribbing")

7 center steek sts

5 = pattern #105
8 = pattern #54
16 = pattern #155
12 = pattern #15

X = (p2, K2b, p2) inc to (p3, k2b, p3) above the "ribbing"

= k1, p1, k2b (from center out) plus 7 steek sts at center front

The numbers in boxes indicate number of sts in patt rep.

105

54

X Filler

155

15

Center Front

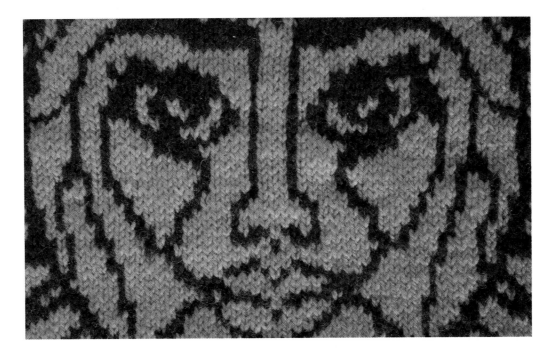

Weeping Sun/Moon

CHALLENGED BY AN IDEA AND SPURRED ON BY the promise of fabulous prizes, Knitting Campers at Sessions 2 and 3 are encouraged to enter an annual knitting contest. One summer I proposed a knitted sun as the subject for the following year's contest. As a steady viewer of the CBS Sunday Morning television program, I had always admired the segue between each story: a close-up of a sun represented in various artistic disciplines: painted, sculpted, modeled, beaded, woven, embroidered, carved, etc. But never had I seen a *knitted* sun. I called CBS, asked to speak to the Guy in Charge of Suns, and was connected to Ken Noble. He was very pleasant and said I should submit some snapshots. So, right after Camp, Chris photographed the winning suns (six from Camp 2 and six from

Camp 3) and we sent them to Ken, who promptly picked three to be mailed to him for taping. They included designs from Linda Lutz, Emily Ocker, and me, and in due course were used on the program. Linda's was particularly splendid and Ken has used it three or four times since.

Anyway, this rambling narrative is leading right where you expect: after knitting up several three-dimensional suns with protruding noses and lace rays, I wondered about a color-pattern sun. This design is the result. Cully was particularly enamored of the original red and black Weeping Sun sweater (which just happens to fit him perfectly) and came up with the idea for a negative-image moon on the second side of the blue and gold one. Okay.

Finished size

46" (117 cm) around; 28" (71 cm) long. To vary the size, alter gauge or weight of wool, or augment/reduce side panel pattern. To shorten or lengthen, add to or subtract from the lower border pattern.

Yarn

Canadian Regal (100% wool; 272 yd/4 oz). 4 skeins each of yellow and grape.

Needles

Approximately size 4 (3.5 mm): 16" (40-cm) and 24" (60-cm) circular. Adjust needle size to obtain desired gauge.

Gauge

20 sts and 24 rows = 4" (10 cm); 5 sts and 6 rows = 1" (2.5 cm).

Body: With 24" (60-cm) needle, cast on 216 sts. The border pattern is 12 sts wide—216 sts gives you 9 repeats. Using the Purl When You Can mode (see page 22) work according to the border chart. Knit 1 rnd, inc as follows: [k9, M1] 24 times being careful not to increase through the side panel pattern

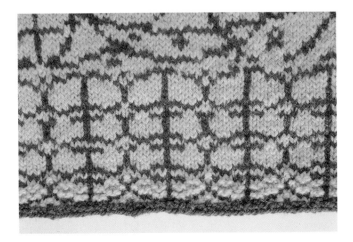

Lengthen or shorten body by adding or subtracting from the lower border.

which continues, uninterrupted, from the cast-on edge—240 sts. Follow the charts to neck opening. Put 33 sts on a thread at center front. Cast on 5 sts for steek and cont around, keeping steek sts in speckles. *Shape neck:* Dec 1 st each side of steek every rnd 6 times—195 sts plus 5 steek sts rem. Work straight to shoulder. Knit 1 rnd plain in whichever color you choose for the shoulder join and place all sts on a thread/holder.

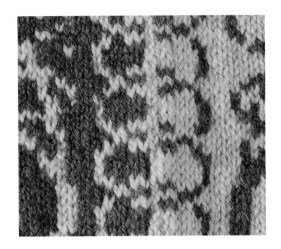

The side panel pattern continues, uninterrupted, from the cast-on edge.

Sleeves: Unable to decide which color the sleeves should be, I made one of each with negative-image cuff patterns. Wacky. With double-pointed needles, cast on 48 sts. Join, being careful not to twist sts. Using the Purl When You Can mode, follow border chart. On next rnd, inc as follows: [K3, M1] around—64 sts. Work straight for 1 to 2" (2.5 to 5 cm). Mark center 3 underarm sts and inc 1 st each side of these 3 sts every 5 rnds until there are 110 sts total. Knit 1 rnd in the color you plan to use for knitting in the sleeve. Place all sts on a thread/holder.

Finishing: Baste down center of neck steek and machine-stitch each side of (and very close to) basting. Cut neck open. Put body flat on a table and line up the top of a sleeve to the shoulder top of body. Mark where the bottom of the sleeve hits the body. Make sure the sleeves match each other, and mark opposite side of body. Baste down center of side panel pattern to depth of sleeve top. Machine stitch

*I joined the shoulders with the 3-needle, 2-st,
I-cord cast-off.*

and cut. Sew up shoulders in whatever manner you like, although I do not recommend weaving because the weight of the sleeve is liable to stretch the shoulder seam. On this model, I used 3-needle, 2-st, I-cord cast-off (see page 15).

Now, you may either cast off the sleeve sts and sew in the sleeves (as for the Lupine cardigan on pages 66–72) or, for a knitted-in sleeve, knit up sts around body armhole, 1 st for each row. You will have more vertical rows than sleeve sts, so with 110 sleeve sts, have 55 on the front and 55 on the back. Calculate how many body sts are to be dec'd and do that as you join the sleeve to the body.

Knit up (and pick up) all sts around neck and work 1 rnd, followed by applied I-cord in the same color. Darn in all ends. Block.

Weeping Sun Sweater

This is nearly the same as the preceding pattern, except I used Québécoise 100% wool (210 yd/3.5 oz: 7 skeins red, 3 skeins black) at a gauge of 5½ sts and 5¾ rows to 1" (2.5 cm). With a size 4 needle, I cast on 210 sts (14 repeats of a slightly different border patt—6 each on the front and back, and one at each side "seam"). I inc'd to 244 sts [k6, M1] 28 times, [k7, M1] 6 times, avoiding working incs along side patts. I put 30 sts on a holder for the neck. I used the crocheted steek (see page 23).

Border chart

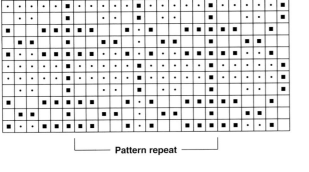

|—— Pattern repeat ——|

■   contrast color

·   purl with background color

☐   background color

Note: For the Sun/Moon, I reversed the colors from front to back. Knitter's choice.

Weeping Sun Chart 1

Continue with Chart 2

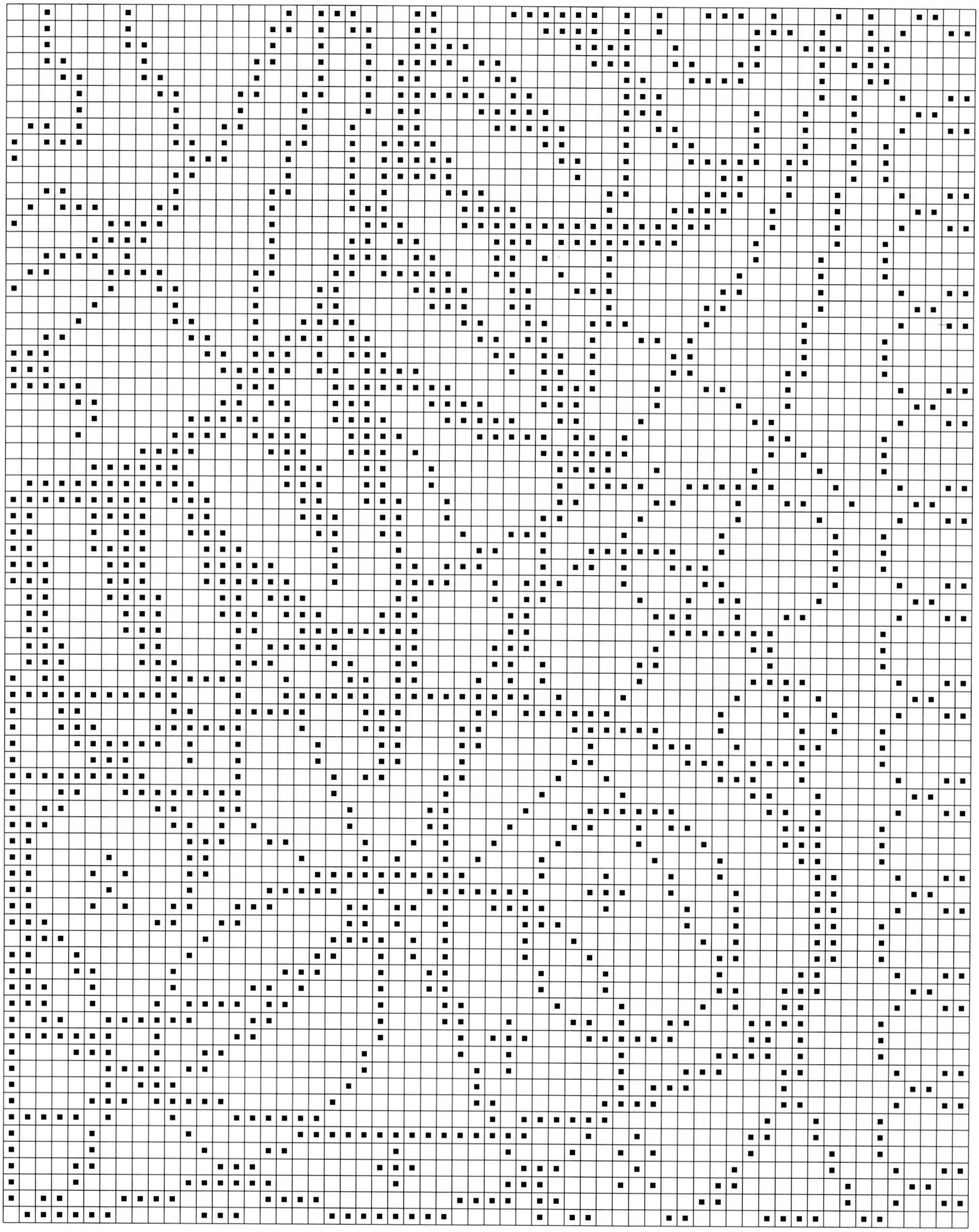

Pivot st

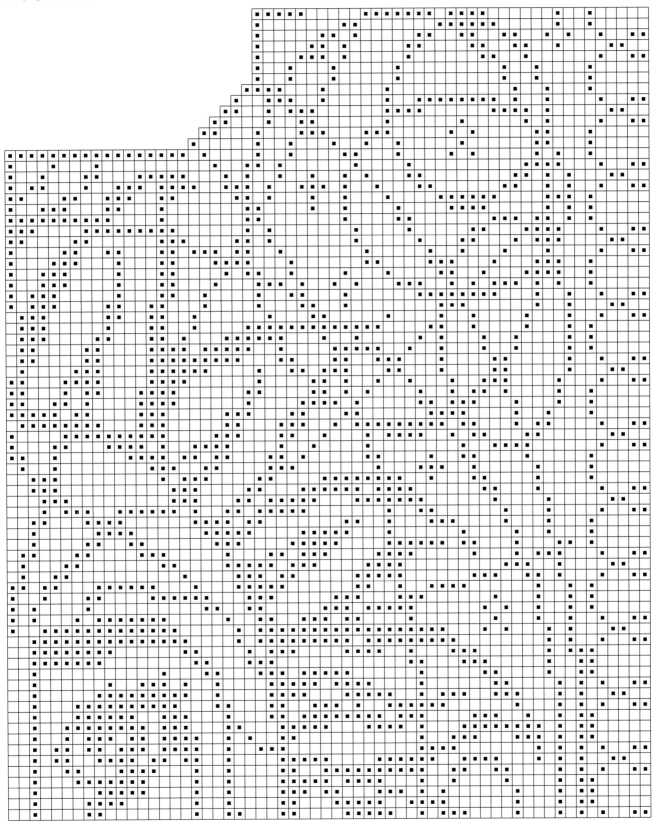

Pivot st

Moon Chart 1

Continue with Chart 3

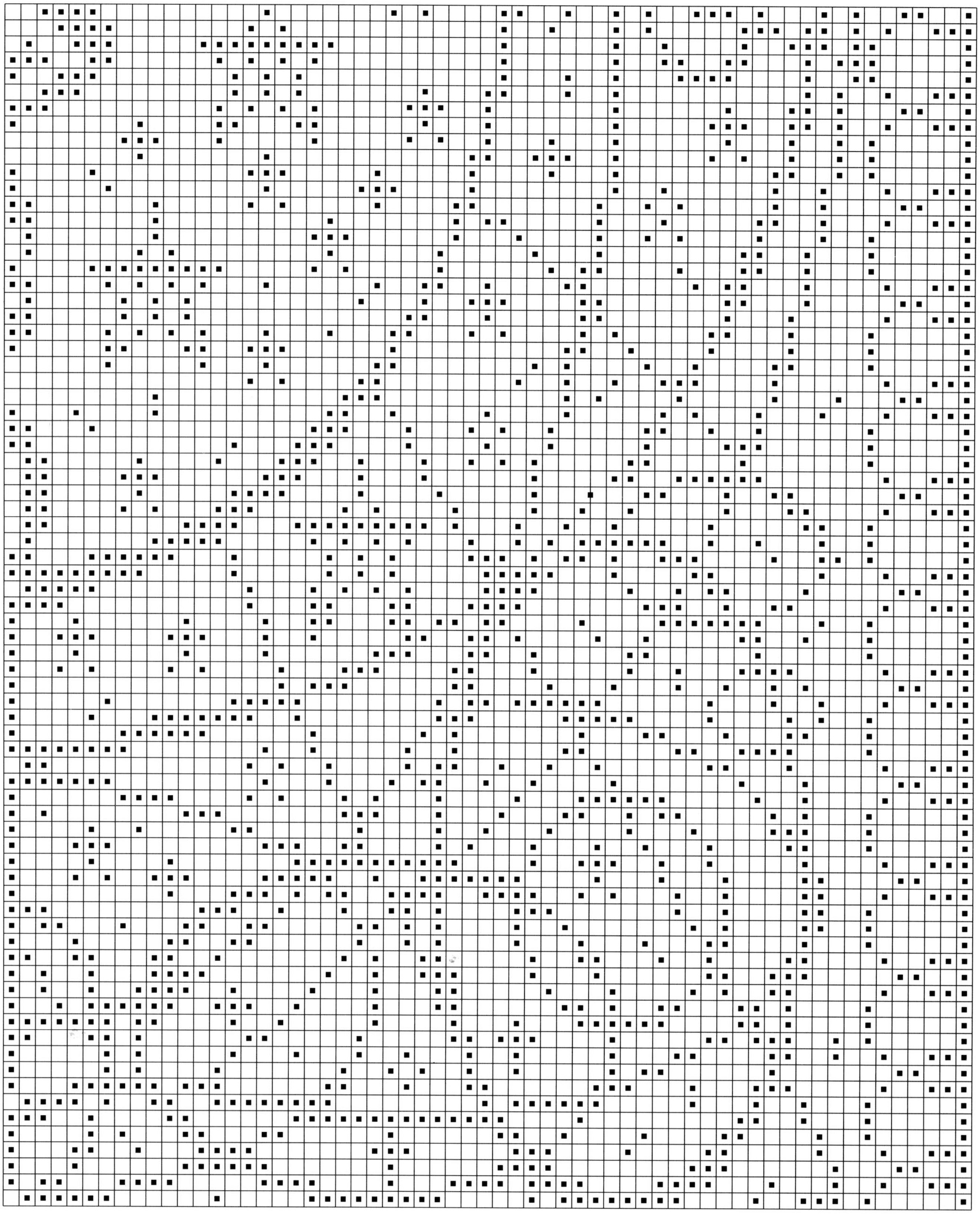

Continue with Chart 2

Continue with Chart 4

Moon Chart 3

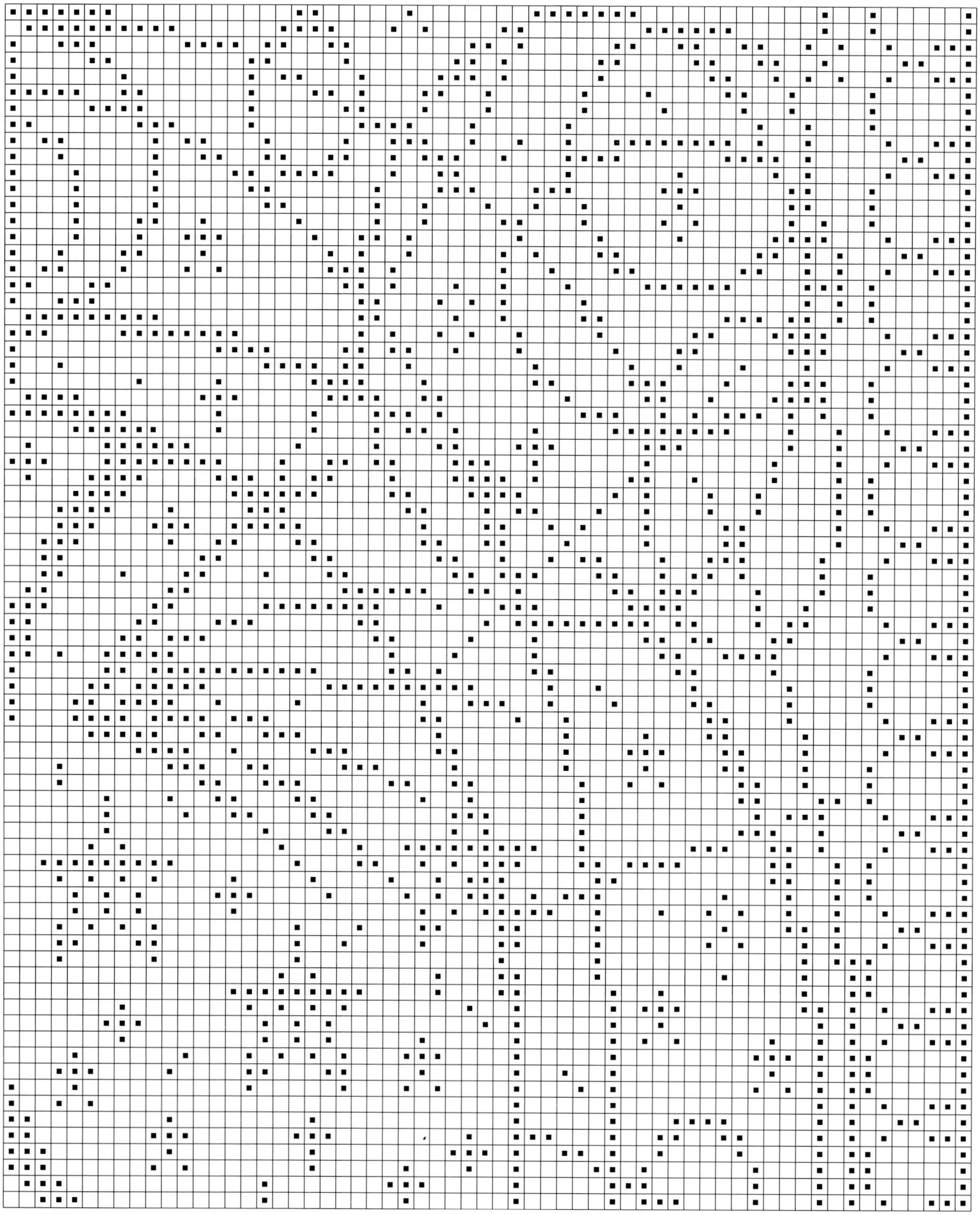

Continue with Chart 4

Moon Chart 4

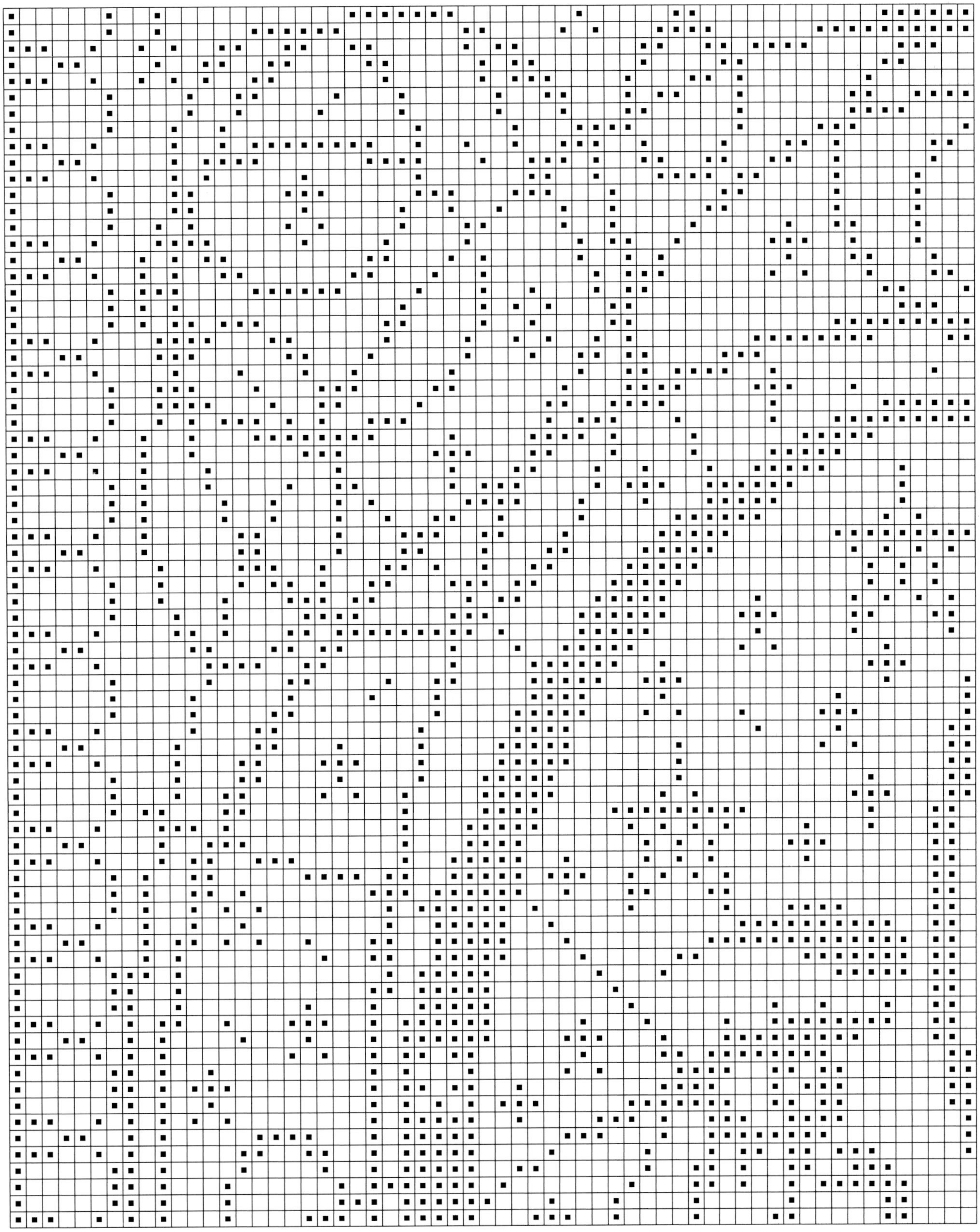

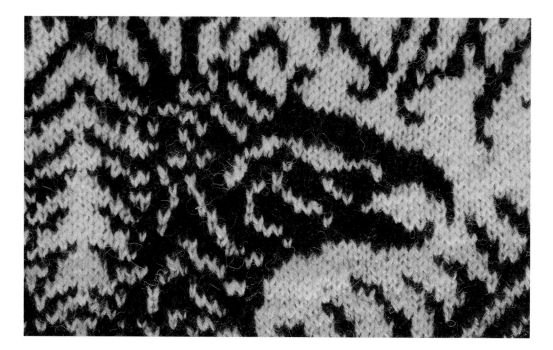

Phoenix Pullover

This chart resulted from playing around on the computer—the Phoenix is two-headed for symmetry. I knitted the color version first, then altered (and I think improved) the chart slightly for the black and gray. It is the revised chart that I offer here; 7 stitches are added to the cardigan for a center steek.

Finished size

44" (112 cm) chest circumference; 31" (79 cm) long. To vary the size, alter gauge by changing needle size or weight of wool or both. To shorten or lengthen, add to or subtract from the lower "flames" border pattern.

Yarn

Shetland wool (150 yd/oz): #134 maroon, 8 oz; #52 fuchsia, #55 burgundy, #1403 custom red, #93 scar- let, #125 persimmon, #129 coral, #FC7 apricot, #90 orange, #66 honey, 1 oz each.

Needles

Approximately size 3 (3.25 mm) for border: 16" (40-cm) and 24" (60-cm) circular, and set of double-pointed (or another circular: see page 20 for knitting with two circular needles). Adjust needle size to obtain the correct gauge. Approximately size 4 (3.5 mm) for body: 24" (60-cm) circular.

Notions

Eleven ½" (1.3-cm) buttons for cardigan.

Gauge

27 sts = 4" (10 cm); 6¾ sts = 1" (2.5 cm).

Note: Near the top of the chart there are some long stretches of carried color. I have tried, whenever possible, to enable you to trap the carried color above a stitch of the same color.

Body: With smaller 24" needle, cast on 304 sts (75 sts in each quadrant plus 4 pivot stitches at centers front and back and at side seams). One line of the chart is read from right to left until you reach the center back of the pullover. Now the pivot stitch is knitted (once) and the same chart line is read from left to right to the halfway point of the round (second pivot stitch). Repeat the foregoing and you are back where you began. Work border chart in the Purl When You Can mode (see page 22). Switch to larger-sized needle and follow the chart, changing colors as inner-directed . . . or not.

Shape Armholes: At about 80 rows from shoulder, put 1 st on a coil-less pin at each underarm. Cast on 5 steek sts and cont around, keeping steek sts in alternate speckles.

On the sleeve I knitted in a line from the W.B. Yeats poem "The Second Coming."

Shape neck: After knitting the top of bird heads, place 65 center-front sts on a thread/holder. Knit 2 final rnds in solid color(s), casting off steek sts. Put all sts on a holder.

Machine stitch and cut armholes (see page 20). Or do as I did and eliminate machine stitching by using the crocheted steek described on page 23. Join shoulder sts with I-cord (see page 15) or plain 3-needle cast-off, which is what I used.

Knit up (see page 19) sts around the armhole (I knitted up 2 sts for every 3 rnds) and then you will know how many sts you will require at sleeve top. Inc sleeve sts to that number.

Sleeve: With dpn, cast on 50 sts. Using the Purl When You Can method, work Border chart until piece measures approximately 5" (12.5 cm) from beg. *Inc rnd:* [k3, M1] 14 times, [k2, M1] 4 times— 68 sts. Knit 5 rnds plain. Mark center 3 underarm sts and inc 1 st each side of underarm (2 sts inc'd) every 6 rnds as follows: *Knit to first marked st, M1, k3, M1. Knit 5 rnds. Rep from * until you have about 100 sts. *Gusset:* Inc 2 sts every 3 rnds until you have 124 sts, or the same number of sts as were knitted up around armhole. (Into the upper sleeve I knitted "Things fall apart; the center cannot hold" from the W. B. Yeats poem, "The Second Coming.") Cont straight until sleeve is desired length.

Knit in the sleeves, matching the technique you used for the shoulder seams.

Finishing: *Neck:* Pick up all sts and work applied 3-stitch I-cord (see page 18) around neck. Add a second layer of I-cord in another color if you like. I didn't. Weave in loose ends. Block.

	background color
	contrast color
	purl in contrast color

Phoenix Chart 1

Continue with Chart 2

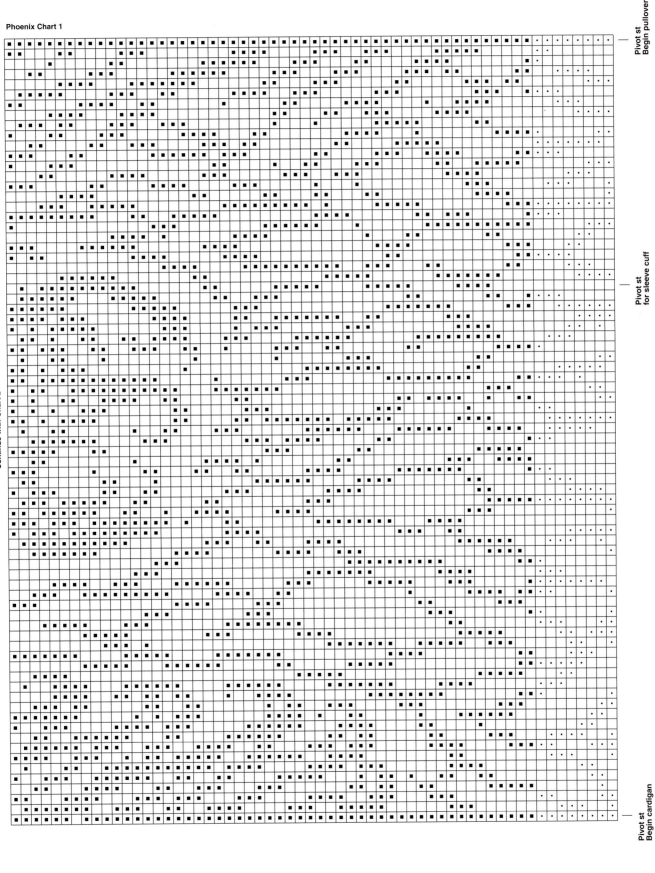

Pivot st
Begin pullover

Pivot st
for sleeve cuff

Pivot st
Begin cardigan

Phoenix Chart 3

Continue with Chart 4

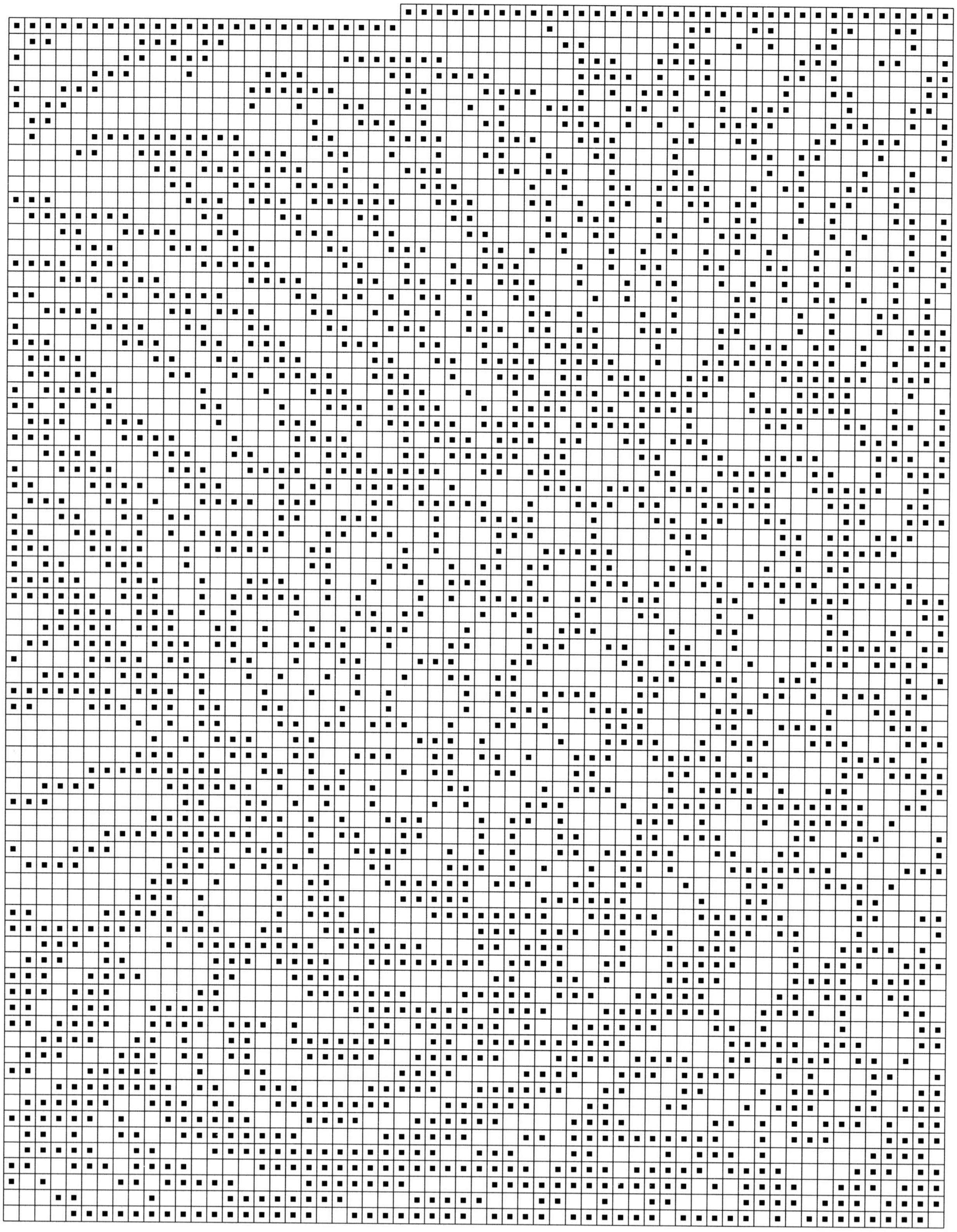

Phoenix Chart 2

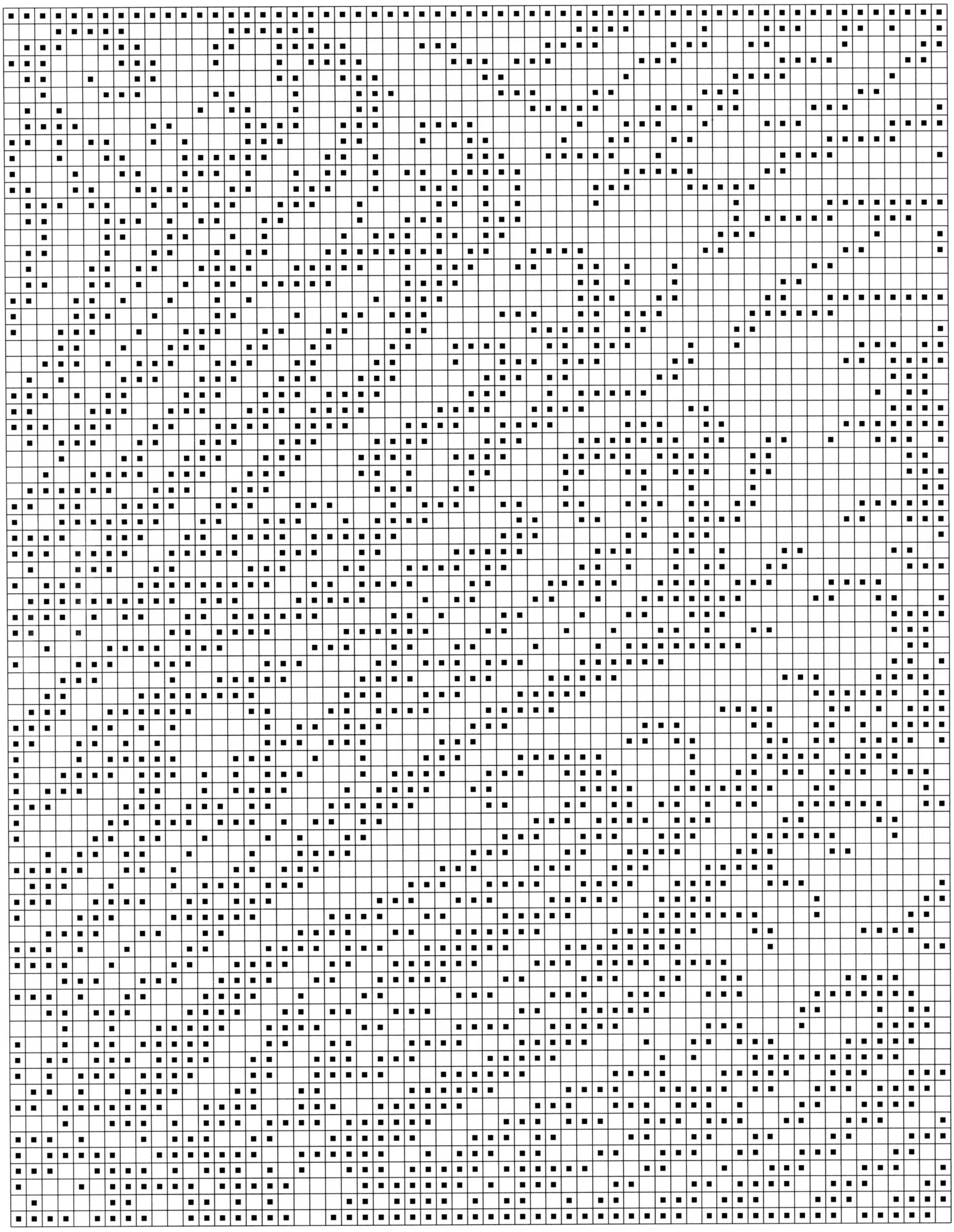

Continue with Chart 3

Phoenix Chart 4

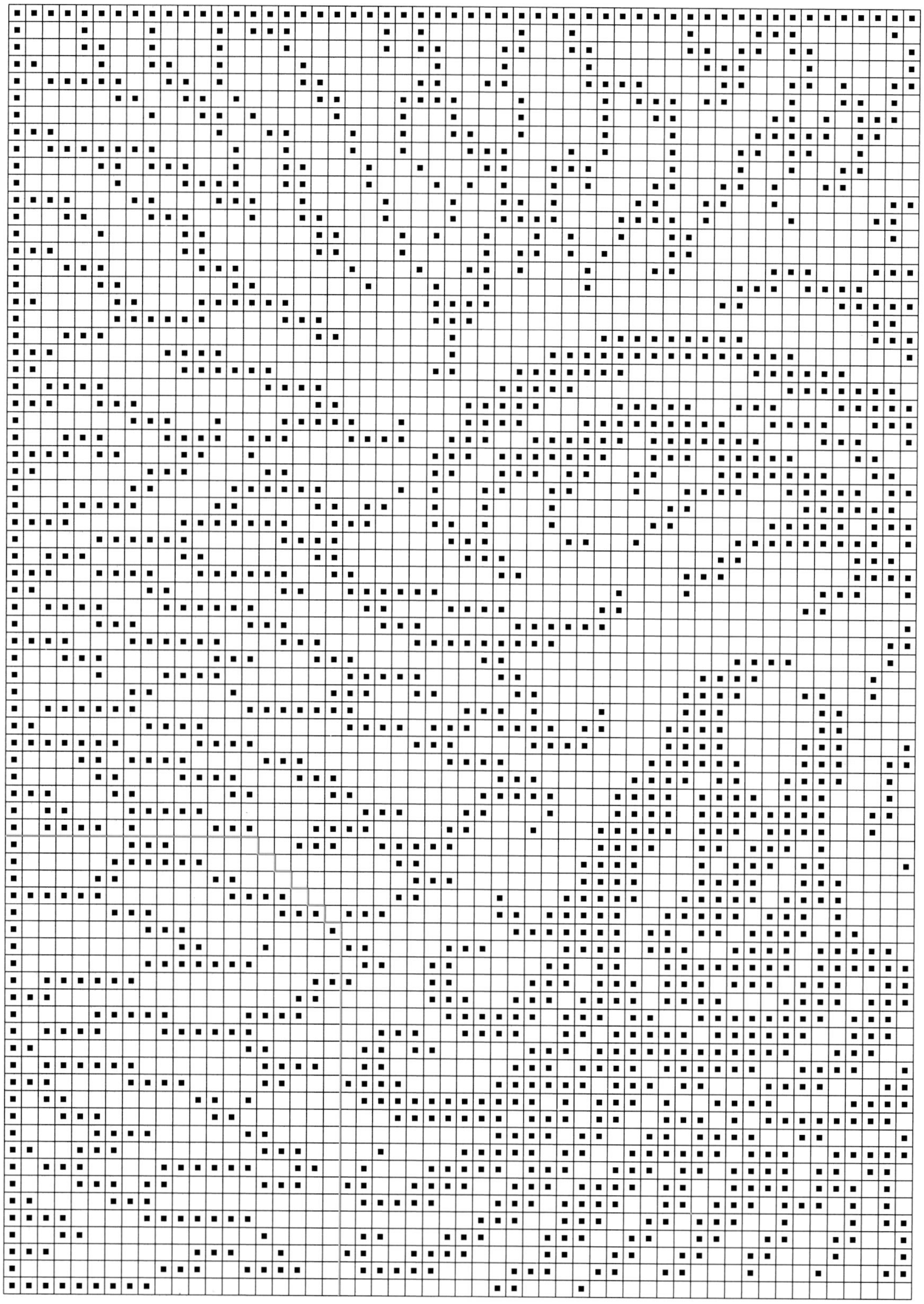

Phoenix Cardigan

Nearly the same as the pullover, the jacket is 34" (86.5 cm) long (extra flames at top and bottom) and is worked in only two Shetland colors: black CC (6 oz) and medium gray MC (10 oz).

Finished size

Same as for pullover.

Body: With smaller cir needle, cast on 312 sts—75 sts in each quadrant, plus 1 pivot st at each side and at center back, plus 7 steek sts, plus 1 knit-up st each side of the steek. The knit-up and pivot sts are kept in black throughout; the steek sts are speckled. One line of the chart is read from left to right until you reach the right side seam. Now the pivot stitch is knitted (once) and the same chart line is read from right to left to the halfway point of the round (second pivot stitch). Repeat the foregoing and you are back where you began. *Neck:* At top of bird head, break wool at center steek. Go back to 22 sts before steek and knit the next 51 sts in MC. Place these 51 sts on a thread/holder. Join CC and cont chart. When you arrive back at center front, cast on 7 new steek sts. **Shape Neck:** *Ssk, knit to within 2 sts of steek, k2tog, knit steek sts; rep from * 5 times. Work straight to shoulder (another 3 rnds for me). Knit a final rnd in black, during which you may cast off the steek sts if you wish. Put all sts on a thread/holder.

Sleeve: Same as for pullover, with shorter cuffs if you want. Another line from the same poem is knitted into the upper right sleeve: "The falcon cannot hear the falconer." Optional, obviously.

Finishing: Baste, machine stitch, and cut both center steeks. With black and beg at lower right corner, pick up 9 sts for every 10 rnds and work applied 3-stitch I-cord (see page 18). After working 6 to 7" (15 to 18 cm), take a look at your work: Is it pulling up? Or sagging? Just right? Adjust needle size or pick-up ratio as necessary. This decision is yours alone; there are too many variables for me to be didactic about an I-cord edging. Turn corner at top

of right side and apply cord to every raw st across the horizontal section and neck side. Dec across neck back as you apply the cord by knitting 2 body sts tog every 4th attachment to prevent the neck back from flaring. Mirror the other side. Go back to lower right corner and apply a bead of gray I-cord on top of the black (using Joyce Williams's method on page 18). At the corner, I swung the gray cord to the inside, between the black cord and the body—then back to the outside at the other corner. (Truth: I was hiding what I considered to be a less-than-beautiful join of cord to raw neck sts. Knitter's choice.)
Buttonholes: During the application of gray cord, insert hidden I-cord buttonholes (see page 18) about every 30 rnds as follows: Knit 2 rnds of unattached I-cord and slip 2 picked-up sts off the left needle. Continue applying. I put in 11 buttonholes.

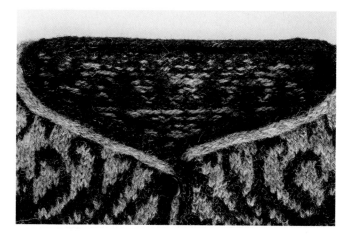

While applying gray I-cord, work hidden I-cord buttonholes.

Apply a third layer of I-cord. I did so in black. Sew on buttons. Tuck under machine stitching and tack down steek for a beautifully neat inside edge.

Mesa Verde Vest

THIS PATTERN WAS INSPIRED BY AN ANASAZI BOWL displayed in the museum of the Mesa Verde cliff dwellings near Durango, Colorado. The bowl was grayish colored clay with drawn black lines. The three-pronged designs (that I call "turkey tracks") were bisected by a slice of zigzags running vertically up each side. Knitting the design causes problems in that the turkey tracks are separated by two rounds of solid color, but the vertical designs are uninterrupted. As you can imagine, there must be a certain amount of breaking and joining wool, accompanied by some muttering. Here is a question that each knitter must decide for him/herself: How much trouble will I go through to achieve a particular effect? In this instance, for me, the effort was worth the result. See what you think as you read through the instructions.

The vest is knitted in the round from the lower edge and includes subtle waist shaping. Armholes and center-front openings are put on a thread and extra steek stitches are cast on for future cutting.

(This and the Navajo vest were originally published in *Knitter's* #21, Winter 1990.)

Finished Size

37 (40, 43)" (94 [101.5, 109] cm) circumference at widest part. Length is up to you. The garment shown is 22" (56 cm) long with a 3½" (9 cm) deep neck.

Materials

Canadian Regal (100% wool; 272 yd/4 oz): MC, 3 (3, 4) skeins; CC, 2 (2, 3) skeins.

Needles

Approximately size 6 (4 mm): 24" (60-cm) circular and pair of double-pointed. Adjust needle size to obtain the correct gauge.

Gauge

20 sts and 22 rows = 4" (10 cm); 5 sts and 5½ rows = 1" (2.5 cm).

Note: Keep the 9 center-front steek stitches in stocking stitch throughout, working alternate colors on pattern rounds.

Body: With MC, cast on 194 (208, 224) sts—185 (199, 215) body sts plus 9 steek sts (to be worked in stocking st every rnd). Join, being careful not to twist sts.

Rnds 1 and 2: *K1, p1; rep from * (keeping center 9 sts in stocking st).

Rnds 3 and 9: *K1 with MC, k1 with CC; rep from *.

Rnds 4, 5, 10, and 11: *K1 with MC, p1 with CC; rep from *.

Rnd 6: *K1 with CC, k1 with MC; rep from *.

Rnds 7 and 8: *P1 with CC, k1 with MC; rep from *.

Rnd 12: K44 (46, 48) with MC, *over next 5 (7, 9) sts knit the MC sts and sl the CC sts*, k87 (93, 101) with CC, rep from * to *, knit with MC to end of rnd.

Rnd 13: K44 (46, 48) sts with CC, [k1 with CC, k1 with MC] 2 (3, 4) times, k88 (94, 102) sts with CC, [k1 with CC, k1 with MC] 2 (3, 4) times, knit with CC to end of rnd.

Vest shown from inside. When working I-cord at the corners, work 3 rows without attaching.

Rnd 14: Work as for Rnd 13, but purl all CC sts.

Pattern set-up: Following chart, work 33 (35, 37) sts in zigzag, 27 (29, 31) sts in side panel, 65 (71, 79) sts in zigzag, 27 (29, 31) sts in side panel, 33 (35, 37) sts in zigzag, and 9 steek sts in alternate colors.

Note: At the end of each pattern band, there is a ridge of CC garter st (knit 1 rnd, purl 1 rnd), *except* through the side panels; there you must add in a length of MC to work the pattern.

Optional waist shaping: Above first zigzag, on first rnd of garter ridge, dec on front and back as follows: *K1 with MC, k2tog with CC; rep from * (do not dec on side panel or steek sts)—151 (163, 174) sts rem. Work 5 more rnds of alternate patt beginning with rnd 4. With CC, inc back to original number by working (k2, M1) across front and back sts on knit row of garter ridge—194 (208, 224) sts.

Cont with pattern sequence (1 zigzag, 1 turkey track, 1 zigzag) until piece measures 12" (30.5 cm) or wanted length to underarm. **Shape armholes:** Place panel sts on threads/holders, and cast on 9 steek sts in their places—158 (168, 180) sts. Cont around until armhole measures 6½" (16.5 cm). **Shape neck:** At center front, place 31 sts on a thread/holder (the 9 steek sts plus 11 on each side of them), cont in patt, and cast on 9 new steek sts when you get back to the center. Work to within 2 sts of center steek, k2tog, k9, ssk. Rep this dec every rnd 7 times—120 (130, 142) sts. Work straight to desired shoulder height (one turkey track on version shown). Place all sts on thread/holder. Machine stitch and cut armholes, neck, and front openings (see page 20).

Finishing: Weave shoulder seams tog with appropriate color for your stopping point. *Armhole border:* With RS facing, place raw underarm sts on a needle and pick up 1 st for each rnd around rest of armhole. With MC, cast on 3 sts. Transfer them to pick-up needle and *k2, sl 1, yo, k1, p2so (the slipped st and the yo). Replace 3 sts to left needle and repeat from *. After a few inches take a look at your work. Is the I-cord pulling up? Drooping? Just right? Adjust needle size if necessary to get the look you want. Cont around entire armhole. Weave end of cord to cast-on edge of cord. *Front Edges:* Work I-cord border as for armholes, with the following additions. *Corners:* Work to corner st, k3 cord sts without attaching, attach corner st, k3 cord sts without attaching, cont around entire front and neck edge. Work a second layer of cord: Choose a vertical row in the finished cord and pick up 1 st for each row. With MC, cast on 3 sts and work as before, adding a hidden buttonhole as follows: At desired buttonhole site, work plain I-cord for 3 rnds, sl 3 picked-up sts off left needle, and begin attaching the cord again. The buttonhole is invisible until used. *Finish cut edges* (see page 72 for cardigan details).

Mesa Verde vest

Turkey track 1

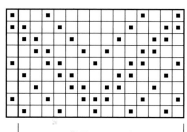

└─ Pattern repeat ─┘

Turkey track 2

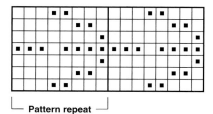

└─ Pattern repeat ─┘

Zigzag

└──────── Pattern repeat ────────┘

Pattern sequence:
Staggered pattern, garter ridge, zigzag, garter ridge, staggered pattern, garter ridge, zigzag, garter ridge, turkey track 1, (garter ridge, zigzag) 3 times, garter ridge, turkey track 2, garter ridge, zigzag, garter ridge, turkey track 1.

The turkey tracks on the right front and back go in the same direction. Turkey tracks on the left front go in the opposite direction.

Side panel - 27 (29, 31) sts

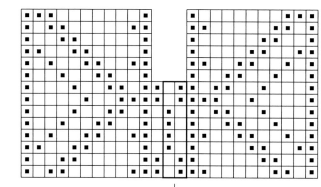

Repeat 2 (3, 4) times

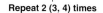

☐ Background color

■ Contrast color

Mimbres Vest

CHRIS AND I HEADED TO THE SOUTHWEST ONE winter to tape another Knitting Vacation video. I was primed with an idea for a color-patterned vest and we had selected shades of Québécoise wool to match the sand and red rocks that we remembered from our last trip to Sedona, Arizona. We flew to Phoenix, rented a car, and headed north. In Prescott, we heard weather reports of snow, but paid little attention and headed for the pass. As we climbed, a gentle snow rapidly turned into a blizzard—inches of snow piled up in minutes. The little rental car was ill-equipped for hazardous duty and we cautiously turned around on the narrow (no guard rail) mountain road and retreated. We felt disappointed not getting to Sedona to match our wool colors, but we hadn't left Wisconsin in February to find snow. So we pointed the car *south* and began filming in Saguaro county.

The design penciled on my graph paper was taken from a small drawing I had seen on a Southwest calendar. The main crisscross in the pattern appealed to me because there was a hiccough in the X; the lines didn't quite mesh in the middle. I began with the X and charted outward, diagonally, in four directions. When I reached the number of stitches I wanted in one quadrant, I mirror-imaged the pattern horizontally to the center back, then mirrored to the other side seam and mirrored back to center front. After each vertical square, I mirrored again in that direction.

Soon I began to lose my original design and could only see the larger picture—just like Mexican ceramic tiles or Victorian knitted bedspreads that form a new pattern from the union of smaller designs.

By now we were in Deming, New Mexico, and decided to visit the Luna County Museum. A new room had been added since we were there last: the Mimbres Room. Into this room we went and were stunned speechless to see, behind a glass case, the very design I was knitting painted in the center of a small bowl. Nearly all the bowls had black paint on sand-colored clay, but this one had *red* paint on sand-colored clay. Uff. The hair prickled on the backs of our necks as we looked at each other and had the same thought: We had been prevented from going to Sedona and had been led to Deming. Nearly all the other bowls in the exhibit had holes punched in the middle of the bottom (to release the spirit of the potter with whom they had been buried?). I was later told that the bowl *without* the hole—the one I was knitting—was "my" bowl and its spirit had not yet been released at my death . . . that was why I was *knitting* it! Uff again!

Deep breath.

If you want a size other than the one in this chart, take the basic square and expand the four diagonals until you have the width you want for one-quarter of the circumference. You may increase/decrease the size in increments of 4 stitches—like the Russian Prime on page 36.

Finished size

44" (112 cm) around at widest part. Length is up to you. The garment shown is 25" (63.5 cm); 14" (35.5 cm) to underarm, 11" (28 cm) armhole, and 6½" (16.5 cm) neck depth.

Gauge

22 sts and 22 rows = 4" (10 cm); 5½ sts and 5½ rows = 1" (2.5 cm).

Yarn

Québécoise (100% wool; 210 yd/3½ oz): beige (MC), 3 skeins; rust-red (CC), 2 skeins. Larger sizes will require 1 more skein each.

Needles

Approximately size 5 (3.75 mm): 24" (60-cm) circular and pair of double-pointed. Adjust needle size to obtain correct gauge.

Body: With MC, cast on 244 ([K]) + 7 steek sts—251 sts total. *Note:* [K] must be divisible by 4. Knit 1 rnd with MC then beg chart. Work until piece measures 14" (35.5 cm), or desired depth to under-

arm (remember that a vest usually has a deeper armhole than a sweater). ***Shape square armhole:*** Centered above the side "seams" at each underarm, place 38 sts on threads/holders. Cast on 7 sts in their place and cont until armhole measures 7" (18 cm). ***Shape neck:*** Place 10% of [K] sts on a thread/holder, plus the 7 center steek sts—12 + 7 + 12 = 31 sts total. Cast on 7 new steek sts and work 1 rnd in patt. Dec 1 st each side of center 7 sts (k2tog, k7, ssk) every 2 rnds 10 times. When you are approx 2" from desired length and beginning a new pattern, change colors for a negative image of pattern. Work straight to top of shoulder. Knit a final rnd in CC (casting off the steek sts if you like). Place all sts on a thread/holder.

Finishing: Machine stitch and cut steek as described on page 20. Work 3-needle, 2-st I-cord cast-off across shoulders (page 15). Apply one layer of CC I-cord around armholes. With main color, knit up one st for each rnd of I-cord. Cast off. Work double I-cord (first layer in CC, second in MC) around entire periphery of garment, picking up the back side of the cast-on edge at the bottom of the garment and incorporating hidden I-cord buttonholes (see page 18) where you like. Block.

I worked the last 2" of patern in the negative.

Hidden I-cord buttonholes may be incorporated where you like and used or not.

Mimbres Vest

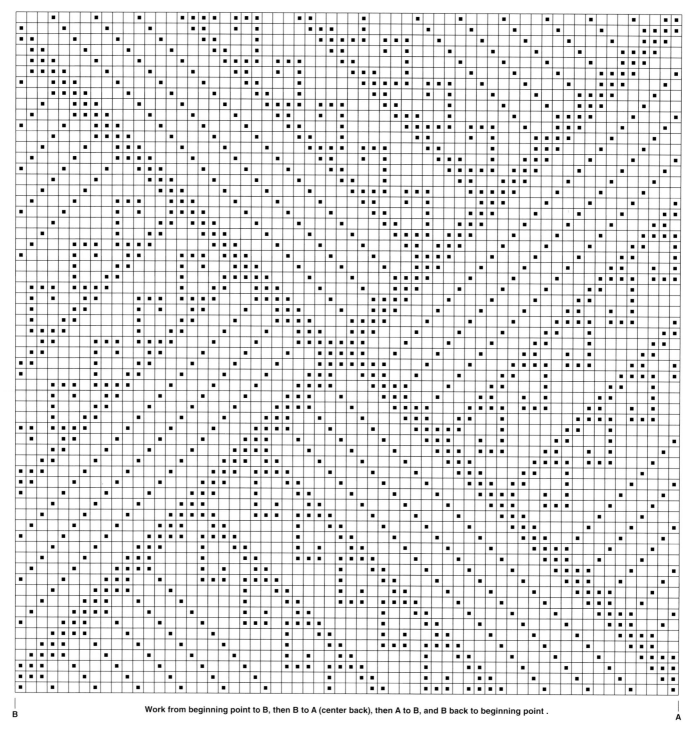

B

Work from beginning point to B, then B to A (center back), then A to B, and B back to beginning point .

A

☐ Background color

■ Contrast color

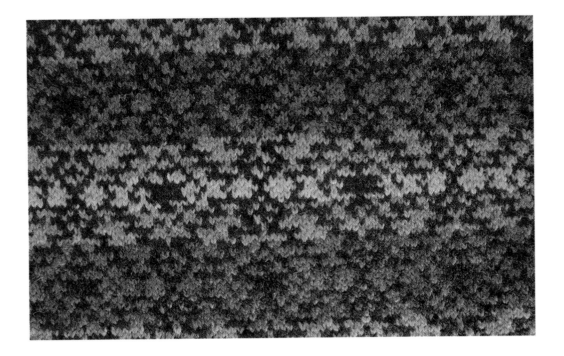

Navajo Vest

THE CONSTRUCTION OF THIS GARMENT IS identical to the Mesa Verde (see pages 125-127), minus the waist shaping. Since the basic shape is so simple, you can make adjustments quite easily. Once you've established your gauge, it is just a matter of measuring the desired circumference of the body, the desired depth of the armhole, how far into the body you want the armhole to be (don't forget to make allowances for your chosen final trim), and where you want the scooped neck to begin.

Now multiply your gauge by the measurement. Divide the 30-stitch pattern repeat into this number, and odds are that it will not divide evenly. Center the pattern in the middle of the back and count, in increments of the pattern repeat, around to the center front. Make sure you have the exact same partial repeat each side of the center front (which will form a nice design of its own), and off you go.

I used 4-oz skeins of Canadian Regal wool: 1 skein each of copper (B), sandstone (C), and rosey beige (D), and 2 skeins live lobster (A). The vest is finished with double I-cord around the armholes, and the bottom is hemmed in the same manner as the Ram's Horn Cardigan on page 86. I also included seven buttonholes which may or may not be used.

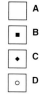

A

B

C

D

Navajo vest

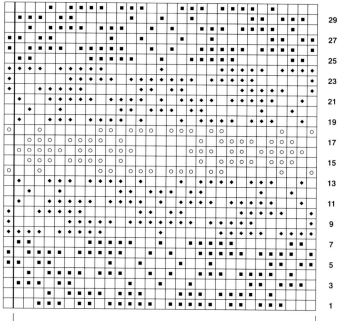

29
27
25
23
21
19
17
15
13
11
9
7
5
3
1

Pattern repeat

I like to finish with shaded hems or hems with messages knitted in.

Stockings with Form-Fitted Arch

THE ORIGINAL STOCKINGS SHOWN HERE ARE ONE of Elizabeth's inspired designs; not as unique as her Wearable Art Stockings (published in *Homespun, Handknit*, Interweave Press, 1987) but more practical in that, knitted in fine wool, they will fit comfortably into a regular shoe. The prototypes were knitted for me in the 1960s (held up by a garter belt!) and are amazingly sensuous as you slip them on and feel the arch shaping snug up into the bottom of your foot.

Elizabeth never made another pair of these stockings. In a thorough search of all her knitting journals, I could find nary a note about this particular design. So I pored over the original, and I think I have it. Points of interest include:

- a tapered leg incorporated into the color or texture pattern
- knitter's choice whether or not to continue the pattern at the ankle
- standard squarish heel flap

- saddle heel turn
- form-fitted arch
- a swath of stocking stitch lovingly wrapped around your metatarsus; a constant stitch count is maintained by simultaneously increasing and decreasing.

Version 1, Aran

This is as close as I could come to Elizabeth's model. It is knitted from the top down and is knee-high. I highly recommend firmly-spun 5-ply authentic Guernsey wool. Not only is it tough and long-wearing, but the firm twist shows off the Sheepfold texture patterns to excellent advantage.

Finished size

Average adult.

Yarn

3 balls Guernsey wool (choose from cream, medium blue, navy, or scarlet. I used Wendy Guernsey.)

Needles

Approximately size 4 (3.5 mm): set of double-pointed (or two 16" [40-cm] circular needles, if you want to knit with Joyce Williams's technique described on page 20). Perhaps a smaller size for the ribbing. Adjust needle size to obtain the correct gauge.

Notions

One spool of nylon thread to strengthen the heel and toe. I use Mettler brand wooly thread nylon which is used on sergers. It comes 330 yd/spool.

Gauge

6½ sts and 8 rows = 1" (2.5 cm) in pattern.

Stitches

Fishbone cable (FB): (worked over 9 sts)
Rnds 1–4: Knit.
Rnd 5: Knit the 4th st, then knit sts 1, 2, 3, and 5, sl 6th st off needle and hold in front of work with thumb, knit sts 7, 8, and 9, then knit st 6.
Rep Rnds 1–5 for pattern.

Sheepfold design (SF):

Elizabeth's original Sheepfold design is charted on page 138. As you become more familiar with it, you will see how easily you may alter the width of the pattern. You may require a wider or narrower calf circumference, or perhaps you choose to work at a different gauge.

M1: Use the increase of your choice.
Leg: Cast on 74 sts. Place marker and join, being careful not to twist sts. Work k1b, p1 rib for just over 1" (2.5 cm). Set-up pattern and inc as follows: K9, p1, k1b, [k4, M1] 4 times, k18, p1, k1b, [k4, M1] 4 times, k9—82 sts. The front Fishbone cable will continue to the tippy toe. The back Fishbone cable will end at the beginning of the heel saddle. Cont as charted, dec 1 st at each SF corner 5 times total—62 sts.

> **It was through this Aran design that** Elizabeth met Barbara Walker. At the end of Walker's first book, *A Treasury of Knitting Patterns*, a note requested additional patterns from readers, which resulted in *A Second Treasury of Knitting Patterns*. Elizabeth submitted her original design for Sheepfold and the two began a long correspondence and friendship.

Heel flap: At desired length to ankle, divide sts in half, with FBs at center front and center back—31 sts each half. Join nylon thread and work back and forth on one set of 31 sts for about 2" (5 cm), cont a vestigial bit of SF on the rem side sts, if desired.

On this heel flap you may opt for the challenge of knitting back backwards (see page 19) where you will figure out how to work knit, purl, twisted knit, FB cable, and traveling sts backward. We take our thrills where we can find them these days.

Heel saddle: At desired heel-flap depth, *knit the 9 FB sts (discontinue FB cable), ssk, turn. With wool fwd sl 1 pwise, p9, with wool fwd sl 2 pwise, turn, k2tog. Repeat from * until all side sts have been consumed. Or don't turn the work but continue thrill-seeking and work forward and backward along the saddle.

Heel gusset: Knit up about 12 to 14 sts along each heel-flap selvedge (depending upon depth of flap) and work 1 rnd on all sts. Keeping gusset sts in purl, mark the corners where the instep meets the gusset and dec 1 st each side of instep every other row as follows: k2tog on right side of instep; ssk on left side. Rep this dec until you have regained the 62 ankle sts (or fewer for a narrow foot).

Loving swath/arch shaping: Mark center st at underfoot and shape each side as follows:

Rnd 1: Work in established pattern to 6 sts before m, k2tog, k3, M1, k3, M1, k3, ssk, cont around foot.

Rnd 2 and all even-numbered rnds: Work in established pattern.

Rnd 3: Work to 7 sts before m, k2tog, k4, M1, k3, M1, k4, ssk, cont around foot.

Rnd 5: Work to 9 st before m, k2tog, k5, M1, k3, M1, k5, ssk, cont around foot.

Rnd 7: Work to 11 sts before m, k2tog, k6, M1, k3, M1, k6, ssk, cont.

Rnd 9: Work to 13 sts before m, k2tog, k7, M1, k3, M1, k7, ssk.

Cont as established and watch the swath spread out across the purl gusset sts and eventually join the stocking-stitch section that edges the FB. Cont shaping until, A) you bump into the FB itself, after which you work straight or, B) you reach 2" (5 cm) from desired total foot length, whichever comes first.

Shape toe: Use your favorite method or work this one: Earmark two 11-st sections fore and aft (the FB and an opposing section at the ball of the foot). Join nylon and *work to within 1 st of m, k2tog, k9, ssk. Work 1 rnd plain. Repeat from * until about 22 sts rem. Line them up parallel to each other and weave toe. (See Kitchener st on page 19.)

VERSION 2
COLOR PATTERN STOCKING

As you can imagine, the above basic instructions apply to this version as well, but switch to a lighter-weight wool because the carried color will double the thickness of the knitting. This points up the advantage of the blue and cream or red and gray stockings: The color pattern ends at the ankle and makes a thinner fabric that fits into your regular shoes with ease. I have used both Shetland jumper-weight (teal and cream and blue and cream stockings) and Icelandic Laceweight (red and gray stockings) with success; for those with sensitive feet, the Shetland is softer. Allow 3 ounces (85 g) of each color Shetland for knee-highs or 50-g balls of each color Spun Icelandic Laceweight wool.

If you follow the color chart for the teal and cream or red and gray stockings, inc to 84 sts after the ribbing. Divide for the heel flap, work saddle heel, and shape foot, making stripe decisions when you're there. It is enormous fun to watch one set of

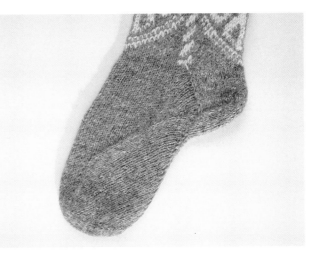

Aran Stocking

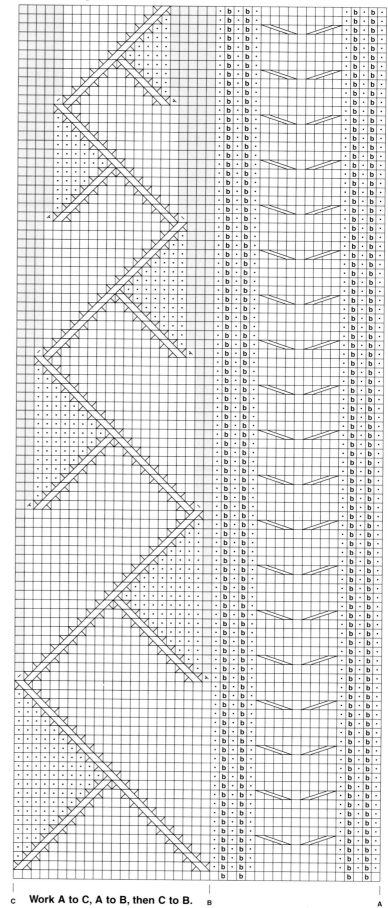

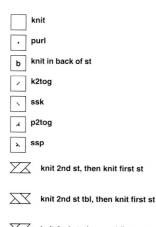

	knit
·	purl
b	knit in back of st
╱	k2tog
╲	ssk
⟋	p2tog
⟍	ssp

knit 2nd st, then knit first st

knit 2nd st tbl, then knit first st

knit 2nd st, then purl first st

purl 2nd st tbl, then knit first st

place first 3 sts on cn to back, k1, k3 on cn, k1, place next st on cn to front, k3, k1 on cn

C   **Work A to C, A to B, then C to B.**   B   A

138   Stockings

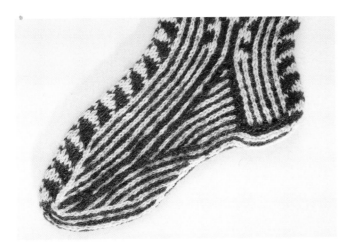

stripes engulf another, and it is advisable to have both stockings going at once: Work a few inches on one, then the other to save having to remember the decisions you made on the first foot.

The red and gray stocking, knitted in Icelandic Laceweight wool, employs what Mary Thomas calls "Festive Knitting" (pages 111–113 of *Mary Thomas's Knitting Book*, Dover Publications, 1972). This back-and-forth intarsia motif is worked in the round as follows: Knit across the instep in light (L) and dark (D). *Drop L and continue around the foot in D. Now, with L hanging from the "wrong" end, knit across instep all D sts of next rnd and slip L sts. Drop D, pick up L and knit back backwards all L sts (while slipping D sts). Drop L. Pick up D (at other end) and knit around foot. Next row: D and L are both poised in the proper place to knit together. Repeat from *. I do not find this to be particularly festive, but it is rather fascinating on a short instep. If you're using Joyce's two circular needles (see page 20), keep instep (pattern) sts on one needle and the rest of the foot on the other, so you can slide from one edge of the pattern section to the other with ease.

Blue and Cream Stocking

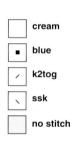

cream

■ blue

╱ k2tog

╲ ssk

no stitch

└─ Left ─┘└────────────── Center panel ──────────────┘└─ Right ─┘
side panel   front/back   side panel

Red and Gray Stocking

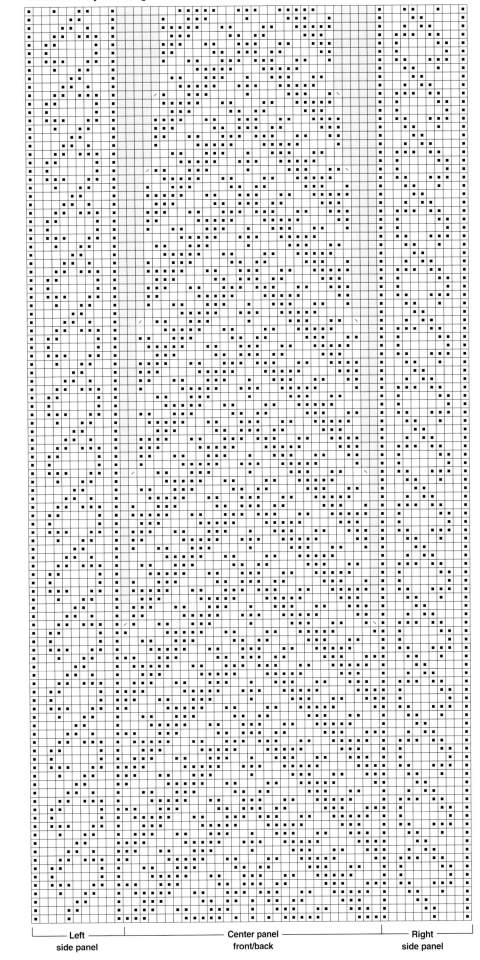

| gray |
| ■ red |
| ╱ k2tog |
| ╲ ssk |
| no stitch |

Left side panel · Center panel front/back · Right side panel

Work right side panel, center front panel, left side panel, then work center back panel.

Stockings with Form-Fitted Arch   141

Teal and Cream Stocking

cream

■ teal

/ k2tog

\ ssk

no stitch

Side panels —————————— Center panel
front/back

Bibliography & Sources

Brunette, Cheryl. *Sweater 101*. Poughkeepsie, New York: Patternworks, 1991.

Debes, Hans M. *Foroysk Bindingarmynstur.* Tórshavn, Faroe Islands: Foroyskt Heimavirki, 1969.

Erlbacher, Maria. *Überlieferte Strickmuster.* Trautenfels, Austria: Schloss Trautenfels, 1986.

Harrell, Betsy. *Anatolian Knitting Designs*. Istanbul, Turkey: Redhouse Press, 1981.

Ligon, Linda ed. *Homespun, Handknit.* Loveland, Colorado: Interweave Press, 1987.

McGregor, Sheila. **The Complete Book of Traditional Fair Isle Knitting*. New York: Scribner's, 1982.

———. **The Complete Book of Traditional Scandinavian Knitting.* New York: St Martin's Press, 1984.

Özbel, Kenan. **Türk Köylü Coraplari*. Istanbul, Turkey: Birinci Baski, 1976.

Snidare, Uuve. **Fiskartröjör och Andra Tröjklassiker. Sweden: Prisma, 1986.*

Spinhoven, Co. *Celtic Charted Designs*. New York: Dover, 1987.

Stanley, Montse. *The Knitter's Handbook.* Pleasantville, New York: Reader's Digest, 1993.

Starmore, Alice. *Alice Starmore's Book of Fair Isle Knitting.* Newtown, Connecticut: Taunton Press, 1988.

Swansen, Meg. *Handknitting with Meg Swansen.* Pitsville, Wisconsin: Schoolhouse Press, 1995.

Thomas, Mary. *Mary Thomas's Knitting Book.* New York: Dover Publications, 1972.

Threads Magazine. *Knitting Around the World.* Newtown, Connecticut: Taunton Books, 1993.

Weston, Madeline. **Classic British Knits*. New York: Crown, 1986.

Walker, Barbara G. *A Second Treasury of Knitting Patterns.* Pittsville, Wisconsin: Schoolhouse Press, 1998.

———. *Knitting From the Top.* Pittsville, Wisconsin: Schoolhouse Press, 1996.

Zimmermann, Elizabeth. *Knitting Without Tears.* New York: Charles Scribner's Sons, 1971.

———. *Knitter's Almanac.* New York: Dover Publications, 1981.

———. *Knitting Workshop.* Pittsville, Wisconsin: Schoolhouse Press, 1981.

———. *Knitting Around.* Pittsville, Wisconsin: Schoolhouse Press, 1989.

Instructional Videos

Cardigan Details (Lupine Cardigan), 90 min
Fair Isle Vest, 90 min
Faroese Sweater, 60 min
Mimbres Vest, 60 min
Russian Prime, 60 min
Saddle-Sleeved Jacket (Bavarian Twisted version) 90 min

Handknitting with Meg Swansen video series:
A Mañanita, 60 min
Dubbelmössa Scarf/Hat, 60 min
I-cord Gloves, 60 min
Puzzle-Pillow Blanket, 30 min
Shawl Collared Vest, 60 min
Sound-the-Bend Jacket, 60 min
Spiral Yoke Sweater, 60 min

Wool Sources

Bartlettyarns, Harmony, Maine. Rangeley and Sheepswool.

Berroco, Uxbridge, Massachusetts. Wendy Guernsey.

Briggs & Little, Harvey Station, New Brunswick, Canada. Canadian Regal.

Brown Sheep Company, Mitchell, Nebraska.

Filiature Lemieux, St Éphrem, Quebec, Canada. Québécoise.

Istex, Reykjavik, Iceland. Icelandic Unspun, Laceweight.

Jamieson & Smith, Lerwick, Shetland Isles. Shetland Wool.

Books marked with an asterisk are currently out of print. At present (1999) all other books, as well as videos, wools and notions, are available from Schoolhouse Press, Pittsville, Wisconsin 54466. (800) YOU-KNIT (968-5648).

Index